D1298440

PHOTOGRAPHY

-IMPROVE YOUR TECHNIQUE-

NEW YORK

Editor: John Farndon

Designer: Eddie Pitcher

Production: Richard Churchill

First published in USA 1985
by Exeter Books
Distributed by Bookthrift
Exeter is a trademark of Simon & Schuster, Inc.
Bookthrift is a registered trademark of Simon & Schuster
New York, New York

ISBN 0-671-07400-8

Printed in Hong Kong

Picture credits
page 5 Shirlene Tucker/Don Hunstein/Colorific; 6 Pete Turner; 7 Tapdance; 8-11 Clay Perry; 12 John Sims; 12(bottom) Vautier/de Nanxe; 13 John de Visser; 14 Ansel Adams; 15 Tessa Musgrave; 16 John Mathers; 17 Mimi Jacobs; 18 Sally and Richard Greenhill; 19 Roger Payling; 20-21 Roger Payling/lens courtesy of Novoflex; 22 Anne Conway; 22-23 Anne Conway; 23-25 Michael Buselle; 26 John Sims; 27(top) Robin Laurence; 27(bottom left) Patrick Thurston; 27(bottom right) Sally and Richard Greenhill; 28(top) Peter Laughran; 28(bottom) Sally and Richard Greenhill; 29 Robin Bath; 30 Laurence Lawry; 30(top) Robin Bath; 31(top left) Don Hunstein/Colorific; 31(top right) Ann Kelly; 32-33 Roger Payling; 34 Nick Holland; 35(top) John de Visser; 35(bottom) Vautier/de Nanxe; 36(top) Dennis Stock/Magnum Photos; 36(bottom left) Steve Herr/Vision International; 36-37 John de Visser; 37(top) Sergio Dorantes; 37(bottom) Timothy Beddow; 38(top) John de Visser; 38(bottom) John Sims; 39(top) Charles Lnears/Atlas Photo; 39(bottom) Anne Conway; 40 Ian Murphy; 41 Jonathan Wright/Bruce Coleman; 42 John Heseltine; 43 Barrie Smith; 44 Sarah King; 45-6 Michael Freeman; 47 Ian McKinnell; 48(top) R. Ian Lloyd/Susan Griggs; 48-9 Dmitri Ilic/Susan Griggs; 49 Tapdance; 49 50(top) Tapdance; 50(bottom) Laurie Lewis; 50-51 Jean-Paul Naiovet/Atlas; 51 Sergio Dorantes; 52-55 Victor Watts; 56(top) David Parker; 56-59 Sally and Richard Greenhill; 60(top) Vautier/de Nanxe; 61(top) Jerry Young; 62(top) Jerry Young; 60-63(bottom) George Wright; 64(top) G. I. Bernard/Oxford Scientific Films; 64-65(bottom) Raj Kamal/Oxford Scientific Films; 65(top) Fleming/Parker; 66(top) Dr Harold Edgerton/Science Photo Library; 66/67(bottom) Fleming/Parker; 67(top) Dr Harold Edgerton/Science Photo Library; 68 Clay Perry; 69(top) John Sims/Vision International; 69(bottom) Martyn Adelman; 70&71(bottom) Clay Perry; 70(top) George Wright; 71(top) Joseph Viest/fotogram; 72-75 Angelo Hornak/location in Hatfield House, by courtesy of Marquess of Salisbury; 76-79 Mike Newton; 80(top) John de Visser; 80(bottom) Ed Baxter/copier courtesy of Ellinchron; 81(top) Jon Bouchier/mirror copier courtesy of Polysales; 81(bottom) Ed Baxter/bellows copier courtesy of Novoflex; 82(top) Jon Bouchier; 82(bottom) Jon Bouchier/zoom copier courtesy of Sunagor; 83(left) Paul Contancio; 83(right) Paul Contancio; 84 Homer Sykes; 84(bottom) John Garret; 85 Richard Houghton; 86(top left) Julian Niemens/Susan Griggs; 86-87 Richard Haughton; 86(bottom) Sergio Dorantes; 87 Richard Haughton; 1900 88 Dave King/copier courtesy of Bush & Meisner; 88-89 Sergio Dorantes; 89(top) Tim Stephens; 89(bottom) Richard Haughton; 90-93 Tessa Musgrave; 94-97 Dave King/equipment courtesy of Transworld Trading; 98-99 Ed Buziak; 100-101 Wayne Gunther; 102 Jerry Young; 103 Paul Brierley.

Artwork credits
page 9 Jeremy Gower; 20 Advertising Arts; 23 Jeremy Gower; 32-33 Oxford Illustrations; 66 Advertising Arts; 91 Jeremy Banks; 92 Bernard Fallon;

INTRODUCTION

In recent years, even the most basic cameras incorporate an impressive array of technological refinements. All but the simplest cameras have some form of exposure metering and exposure automation. Many focus automatically. And some will even load the film and wind on for you as well. These sophisticated aids mean that you can get satisfactory results most of the time without really thinking. But there is a yawning gap between 'satisfactory' results and quality photographs. This book aims to help you bridge that gap.

A vital element in quality photography is accurate exposure, and the book opens with a section on precision exposure techniques. The photographer is shown how to hand-hold meters for controlled light readings. The use of incident readings, key tones, grey cards and other systems that help you match the light on the subject to the exposure characteristics of the film, are also fully explained—along with a few useful shortcuts. And there is a clear introduction to the famous 'zone' system.

But it is the photographer's handling of light which is the key to success, and three full chapters are devoted to making the most of the light available—and how to create your own light. You are shown how to get good results whatever the weather, how to cope with light sources in the picture, how to get natural-looking pictures whatever the light, flashgun and many other techniques. A chapter on high-speed flash provides all the information you need to amaze your friends with bullet-stopping shots.

What all these techniques demand, above all, is meticulous care and attention to detail. While there is no need to spend days or even months over a single shot, like some professionals do, a thorough and precise technique will be amply rewarded by the sparkling, high-quality results you achieve every time.

CONTENTS

Chapter 1

PRECISION PHOTOGRAPHY
Controlled exposure

By far the most important element in high quality picture-taking is precise exposure. All films will tolerate a certain amount of error in exposure. With black and white films, the margin for error is quite considerable; with colour transparency film it is very small. But only if the exposure is exactly right will the film yield its full potential.

Modern exposure meters and automatic exposure systems ensure that most photographers achieve results that fall well within the film's exposure latitude nearly all the time. However, very few achieve the precision exposure needed for quality results. It is this slight inaccuracy in exposure that often distinguishes the work of the amateur from that of the professional.

Heavy under- or overexposure is easy to recognize. In negatives, pale shadows and virtually transparent highlights with no detail clearly indicate underexposure. In a slide, such symptoms signify overexposure. Similarly, a dense, dark negative has been overexposed while a dense, dark slide is underexposed. Slight inaccuracies in exposure, however, are less easy to identify, particularly if you have nothing to make a comparison with.

The ability to recognize perfect exposure at a glance comes only with experience, but you can begin to get an idea of how exposure affects film by making a series of tests with your favourite films in a range of typical situations. Set the camera on a tripod to ensure that the pictures are perfectly sharp whatever the shutter speed. If the camera is automatic, set the exposure controls manually. If the camera has no manual override, control the exposure by altering the film speed dial. Take a meter reading and make a series of exposures at different aperture settings either side of the indicated exposure.

Start with four stops less exposure than indicated and gradually increase the aperture by a third of a stop for each consecutive frame until you reach four stops overexposure. You may have to alter the shutter speed to give the full range of apertures either side of the indicated exposure. Try this experiment with a number of different subjects, in a range of different conditions. Careful examination of these test rolls should reveal a great deal about the relationship between exposure and film performance.

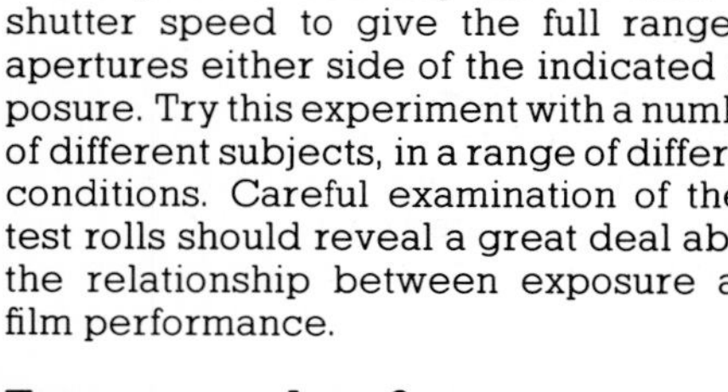

Exposure and performance

Colour slide film, as your tests should demonstrate, needs very accurate exposure indeed. But it tolerates underexposure better than over exposure. This is because in an overexposed slide, the reversal process removes too much of the coloured dye that makes up the image, so that shadows are pale and thin and highlights are bleached out completely. Nothing can be done to restore this lost dye.

When the slide is slightly underexposed, however, too little dye is removed. Shadows are very dense and even highlights are a little thick. But the image dye is still present, and by looking at the slide against a very bright light, it is possible to see the full range of colour and detail. This

Sunshade ***Underexposure by half a stop helped to give the blue and red, so important in this picture, the maximum saturation.***

Bob Marley ***A good overall exposure reading of a brightly lit stage can be taken by briefly pointing an incident meter into the stage spotlight beam***

is only true for limited underexposure—perhaps one stop—and heavily underexposed slides are useless. But a little underexposure can actually improve some slides because the thick image dyes give rich, saturated colours. Indeed, slides intended for reproduction in print are nearly always underexposed by a ⅓ stop and then printed correctly.

Many photographers prefer to 'underexpose' slide film by perhaps half a stop for nearly all their pictures because they like the slightly richer colours this gives. If your camera is automatic, you can achieve the same result simply by setting the film speed 30% less than recommended.

Colour negative film, on the other hand, will tolerate much wider errors in exposure. Yet while it can be overexposed perhaps as much as three stops and still give acceptable prints, it can take little underexposure. This, of course, is because with negatives it is underexposure which removes too much dye, not overexposure. So with negative film, both colour and black and white, the aim is normally to bias the exposure towards the shadows in the picture while slide film is biased towards the highlights.

Hand-held meters

To achieve accurate exposure, you must be able to measure the amount of light in the scene exactly and, nowadays, most new cameras have built-in exposure meters. Built-in meters undoubtedly help even the most inexperienced photographer to achieve good results in most situations, but there are occasions when it pays to use a separate hand-held meter.

Hand-held meters are intrinsically no more accurate than built-in meters and measure light in much the same way. The difference comes in the way photographers tend to use them.

With a built-in meter, the normal technique for taking a reading is simply to line up the camera on the subject as if you were going to take a picture. The meter then gives a general reading for all or part of the scene you can see through the viewfinder—depending on whether the meter is *overall, centre-weighted* or *spot*.

This system is quick and easy to use and gives good results most of the time. However, it is only reliable if there is a fairly even mixture of tones in the scene—some dark, some light, some in between—with no particular extremes. More significantly, perhaps, it also assumes that all or a large part of the scene is equally important and that there are no small areas of interest. With centre-weighted and spot meters the middle of the picture has more effect on the reading, but even with these the 'read' area is large.

A hand-held meter encourages far greater care in exposure although it takes longer to use. It encourages you to not only make the general reading that you make with the built-in meter, but also to single out areas within the scene and meter them individually. There are a number of other special metering techniques that can be used to ensure correct exposure and all are easier with a hand-held meter.

It is possible to practise these special metering techniques with a built-in meter, but it is generally more awkward. It would be a nuisance, for instance, to have to unclamp your camera from a tripod to make special readings. Similarly, because you have to put your eye to the viewfinder to read a built-in meter, special readings can be physically awkward—to take a light reading for a portrait 10 cm away from someone's face, you actually have to stand that close. Indeed, some metering techniques, such as incident light metering (see above), cannot be done with a built-in meter without a little trickery.

For the special metering techniques outlined here, then, you should use a hand-held meter. You can use a built-in meter, but this makes life difficult and may tempt you to make short cuts.

Light background *Taking an exposure reading from a light background can lead to underexposure, left. A built-in meter 'sees' the background as a brightly lit grey surface. A shot with incident metering, right, gives better results*

Dark background *The opposite problem occurs with a dark background, left. Reflected light meters cannot be relied on to determine correct exposure, but incident meters are unaffected by subject reflectivity*

Average background *A subject with an average range of tones is interpreted similarly by both incident and reflected light meters*

Exposure

Although the precision of the light meter may lead you to believe that there is only one 'correct' exposure for every scene, exposure is often very much a compromise. Normally, the aim is to record detail in every part of the scene, both shadows and highlights, including all the tones between white and black that correspond to the tones in the original scene.

However, the human eye can cope with shadows and highlights far better than a film can. While the human eye will see detail in both shadows and highlights when the highlights are 1000 times as bright as the shadows—a brightness range of 1000 : 1—a black and white film can only cope with a range of 128 : 1.

You can use a hand-held light meter to see if the brightness range is too great for the film to cope with. Move into the scene and take a reading from the lightest part of the subject and then the darkest. If the difference between the two readings is more than seven *f*-stops, the brightness range is too great for black and white film to cope with. This does not mean that you cannot take your picture. It simply means that you must compromise and decide whether to overexpose the highlights or underexpose the shadows.

Colour print film can show detail in dark and light areas with about seven stops difference in brightness. Colour slide film can only manage a five stop range of brightness.

Inevitably, then, some of the detail the photographer sees in the original scene must be lost. Just what is lost depends upon the exposure. If you give a short exposure, shadow detail will be lost; if you give a long exposure there will be good detail in the shadows but the highlights will be 'burnt out'.

For black and white film, the traditional method is to expose for the shadows and let the highlights take care of themselves—that is, exposure is the minimum necessary to give good detail in the shadows. This does not mean that you take your meter reading from the shadows only, but simply that it is normally preferable to allow the highlights to burn out a little in order to get good detail in the darkest areas.

This policy works reasonably well for colour negative film as well, but not for colour slide film which gives unpleasant desaturated colours in the highlights when it is overexposed. Exposure for slides, therefore, is normally biased toward the highlights.

The exposure should really be chosen to give the sort of photograph you want. If you want detail in the highlights most, expose for these; if you want shadow detail picked out, expose for these. Once you have decided what you want, you can use a hand-held meter to help you establish what exposure gives you the effect you want.

Reflected light

Like built-in meters, most hand-held meters are designed to measure light reflected from the subject. These meters are referred to as *reflected light* meters. *Incident light* meters are also available and they are used to meter light incident (falling) upon the subject rather than reflected from it. Some meters can take both reflected and incident light readings. The procedure for taking a reading varies from meter to meter and you should refer to the manufacturer's instructions.

Reflected light readings can be taken in a number of ways, the most common of which is a general reading similar to the reading you take with a built-in meter. The meter is simply held next to the camera and pointed at the subject. Because the meter responds to exactly what the camera records—the light reflected from the subject—this method normally gives good results.

You should check, however, that the meter has a similar angle of acceptance as the angle of view of the lens on your camera. Typically the meter's angle of acceptance is about 45° which corres-

Pointing the meter *Unlike a built-in meter, a hand-held meter does not make allowances for bright skies. For accuracy, aim it slightly downwards*

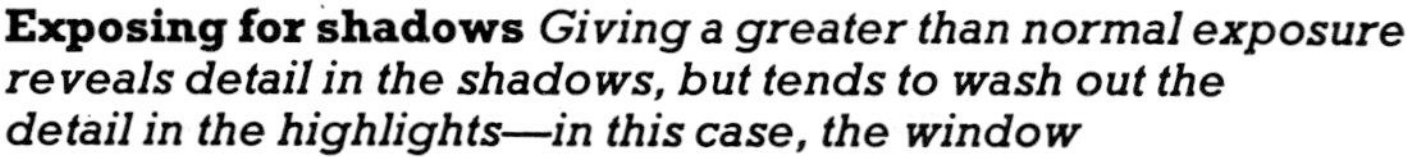

Exposing for shadows *Giving a greater than normal exposure reveals detail in the shadows, but tends to wash out the detail in the highlights—in this case, the window*

Exposing for highlights *With a shorter exposure, detail in the highlight areas is visible and colours are more saturated but shadow and midtone detail are lost*

ponds to the angle of view of a standard 50 mm lens. You should bear this in mind when changing lenses. While a TTL meter automatically adjusts for different lenses, a general scene reading with a hand-held meter may give incorrect exposure when you have anything but the standard lens on the camera.

Nevertheless, as long as direct sunlight does not catch the meter cell—shade it with your hand if necessary—a general scene reading gives acceptable exposures for most subjects. However, it is worth examining the scene to see if you might improve your results by exposing for particular areas.

Tilting the meter

Landscapes, for example, and indeed other photographs, often include a large sky area. This has a considerable influence on general scene readings, and you may get two widely different readings with two similar views, simply because you include different proportions of sky. If you include a large area of sky in the frame, shadow detail could be lost on the ground if you only take a general scene reading.

Whether it is a landscape or a building you are shooting, aim the meter down towards the ground to get your reading. Start with the meter towards the sky and slowly tilt it downwards. The reading will drop rapidly at first and then become steady once all the sky is excluded. If you use this steady reading directly for your exposure, the sky may well be a little burnt out. Unless you want a featureless sky, therefore, you should expose at one stop less than indicated.

Closing in

When the main point of interest is fairly small in the frame—a small figure against a seascape, for instance—a general scene reading may again give an unsatisfactory reading since it will be influenced mostly by the brightness of the sea. In this instance, move in close to take a reading directly from the figure.

Portraits particularly benefit from this metering technique, whether outdoors or in the studio. Your reading should be taken with the meter held at a distance of 15 cm in front of the subject's face.

Out of doors, close-up meter readings may sometimes give false results if your point of interest is some distance from the camera. Haze between the camera and the subject can result in overexposure, especially on a sunny day. So you should again expose at one stop less than the close-up reading indicates.

Key tones

Areas that are coloured very dark or very light can also fool a reflected light meter. Even under identical lighting conditions, a meter will indicate that more exposure is needed for a very dark coloured object than for a very light coloured object. This is because dark colours reflect less light than light ones. A meter simply indicates that there is less light, without showing why. If you follow the exposure indicated by

Compromise exposure *Taking an exposure reading from a middle tone gives an exposure that fully exploits the contrast range of the film*

the meter, therefore, a black curtain would be rendered grey in the final photograph. To keep the curtain black, you must use an exposure that is less than that indicated by three or four stops.

A white subject, on the other hand, may need three or more stops exposure than that shown. Learning to predict whether or not you need to adjust the recommended exposure, and by how much, only takes a little experience. For mainly dark subjects, you should normally give less exposure than the meter suggests by using a smaller aperture or a faster shutter speed or both. For mainly light subjects the opposite is true.

Tone cards

One valuable technique for ensuring that important areas of the picture are correctly exposed, whether in shadow or light, dark or light coloured, is to measure exposure against a reference tone.

This reference tone may be anything that corresponds to the subject. If shooting distant grassy hills, for instance, you can point the meter at the grass nearby. Providing the lighting is identical, the meter reading for the grass gives the right exposure for the distant hills.

Similarly, you can point the meter at your hand to get a reading for a portrait—again providing the lighting on the hand is identical to the light on the subject. This can be useful when shooting in a hurry or when you cannot move near enough to the subject to take a close-up reading. Many news photographers prepare their exposure in this way, while waiting for a celebrity to emerge from a building.

One of the most useful reference tones is a grey card and Kodak produce a neutral, 18 per cent reflector card for just this purpose. In the final picture, this card would come out medium grey if given the correct exposure. Exposing for this grey card gives a good range of tones either side of a medium grey. It may miss out on detail in the extreme highlights or dark shadows, but ensures that the negative is neither very thin nor very dense.

Some photographers also use a white card in some circumstances. This provides a highlight reading. The highlights will be properly exposed on black and white film if you give about 3 stops more exposure than indicated when you point the meter at the card. It may be particularly valuable when using colour slide film and helps to avoid overexposing the highlights. It can also be valuable in very low light conditions when your meter is insufficiently sensitive to give a reading.

Subject brightness range

Exposure adjustment in f-stops	Brightness level	Typical subject
+3	Diffuse highlights	White clouds, snow, white paint
+2	Light tones	Very pale skin, light blue sky, dry white sand
+1	Medium light tones	Pale skin, weathered wood, foliage, red brick, deep blue sky
0	Middle grey	Kodak neutral test card
−1	Medium dark tones	Dark skin, dark foliage, tree trunks
−2	Dark tones	Very dark skin, most dark clothing
−3	Very dark tones	Textured black objects
−4	Black	Untextured black

To use this table, take a light reading from a subject of about the same tone as one of those listed in the right-hand column. The exposure adjustment that needs to be applied to correctly expose the subject is listed in the left-hand column. These figures are only approximate and may vary in individual cases.

Advanced metering

Experienced photographers often use complicated systems to determine the correct exposure. Such methods as the Zone System and the YOB System are ways of working out the precise effects of exposure on the final picture. These systems will be dealt with more fully later, but in general they mean taking several brightness measurements from various parts of the scene, usually with a spot meter that takes exposure readings from a very small area. The different brightnesses of the scene are then related to the way they will appear in the final print or slide.

For example, if the photographer knows that pale skin tones usually look best in the print if they have been given twice as much exposure as a neutral subject, such as a Kodak grey card, then he can simply take a reading from a skin tone and set an exposure that is one stop higher than that indicated by the meter. With the exposure needed for this important tone known, the photographer can then determine which other tones will be over- or underexposed. Then, adjustments to the composition of the picture or the lighting, if some important detail of the subject needs to be brought into the brightness range of the film, can be made. More advanced applications of these methods may even involve adjustments to the development time given to the film in order to adjust the contrast of the picture. The accompanying table uses information determined by Kodak, and shows the relative brightness of several subjects lit by the sun. Use the table to work out the exposure compensation you need to apply to a meter reading from any part of your subject.

Silhouette *There is often no 'right' exposure—it is for the photographer to decide whether he wants shadow detail or a strong silhouette*

Street scene *Sometimes you have to accept overexposure of highlights and loss of highlight detail in order to achieve the best possible shadow detail*

Don't stick to these recommendations too rigidly; they are only meant as guidelines. Remember, there are occasions when you may want to underexpose the sky to give full colour saturation. Similarly, you may want to overexpose a dark subject to reveal textural details.

An essential part of any advanced metering method is being able to imagine what the effect of the exposure is going to be—that is, the ability to *previsualize* the result. This is, of course, affected by the film. But even the equipment itself can affect the result, and you must know what effects your lenses and shutters have so that you can make allowances for them. This can only be done by trial and error, and by carefully evaluating your results. But there are certain factors you should look out for.

The accuracy of your shutter speeds may vary, depending on the speed set. To take a common example, the 1/500 second top speed of a leaf shutter is frequently nearer 1/350 second. Lenses also vary in the amount of light that they transmit. Zooms in particular tend to transmit less light than is suggested by the marked *f*-numbers.

These equipment variations added to variations in meters and personal techniques mean that it is by no means unusual for serious photographers to find that manufacturers' recommended film speeds do not work for them. With 64 ASA (ISO) Kodachrome, for example, it is common to find people using an exposure index of 50 or 80. With black and white films still wider variations are found.

This 'fine tuning' of film speeds does not mean that there is anything wrong with either you or your equipment. It simply means that your working methods, your subjects, and the equipment and materials you use require a slight variation from the standard.

Using the meter

Once you know how your film and equipment affect the picture, and have determined suitable exposure indices for your type of work, you can use this information when metering.

There are four basic types of metering—reflected light readings, incident light readings, brightness range method and keytone metering. The way these are used for most conditions is described in the previous pages, but for unusual conditions, these techniques must be adapted.

The reflected light method is where the meter is pointed directly at the subject to measure the light reflected from it. The simplest way to use reflected light readings is to use the averaging method (see page 9). But if the subject contains large dark areas, the exposure should be halved by using the A setting on the meter. In scenes with large expanses of light tone the exposure should be increased—the C setting is

Castle *Deliberate underexposure—here by one stop—often helps to ensure good colour saturation and is particularly useful in bright, harsh sunlight*

usually adequate.

For colour photography, the incident method is often preferable. This measures the light falling on the subject, and so is not affected by the tone of the subject. Under most circumstances this gives reasonable and realistic tone reproduction, especially with backlit subjects. But in subjects with plenty of specular highlights, such as the sun reflected off water, slightly less exposure is usually preferable in order to give some detail in the highlights. This is especially true with transparency film where burnt-out highlights rarely look good. Using the A setting in these conditions should improve results.

Incident light readings are usually taken using a diffuser dome over the meter cell. If your meter does not have one of these, you can take a reflected light reading from a standard 18 per cent grey card. Should you find yourself in the situation that you want to take an incident reading, but have neither a diffuser dome nor a grey card, then use a piece of white card or paper, using an ASA setting on the meter equal to the speed of the film divided by five.

Selective metering

The methods mentioned so far involve very general readings of the subject and light. But for more critical work it is better to take reflected light readings from specific parts of the subject.

The simplest of these methods—the brightness range technique—involves taking a close-up reading from the brightest part of the subject, and a similar reading from the darkest part, making notes of the exposure values each time. The main exposure index (the main arrow) is then placed half way between the two readings. This ensures that the brightness range of the subject falls at the mid point of the exposure range of the film, so that there is no unnecessary loss of detail in shadows or highlights.

The film latitude is shown by the U and O marks—a range of seven stops. This is intended primarily for black and white work, so for use with colour transparency the range should be reduced to five stops by using the next set of marks.

Sometimes the brightness range in the subject may be too great, in which case you will have to sacrifice some detail—either in the shadows or the highlights. If the highlight detail is most important, then take a reading from the brightest diffuse tone and set the O position opposite the given reading. If shadow detail is more important, then use a similar procedure, metering from the darkest tone and using the U setting. The U setting can also be used with films (usually black and white) which have a long tonal range. This is an alternative to the previously mentioned brightness range method. With long tonal range films, the highlight detail is not sacrificed, but metering from the darkest tone and using U gives good shadow detail in the final picture.

Another reflected light technique is the key tone method. This is where you meter from an area which you want to appear as a mid tone in the final picture. If, for example, you want a skin tone to appear as a mid grey, you simply meter from the skin and use the main index on the meter dial. Variations are also possible using the other marks. You might decide that skin tones look better if they are one stop lighter than mid grey, in which case you could use the C mark.

Settings on the Weston meter

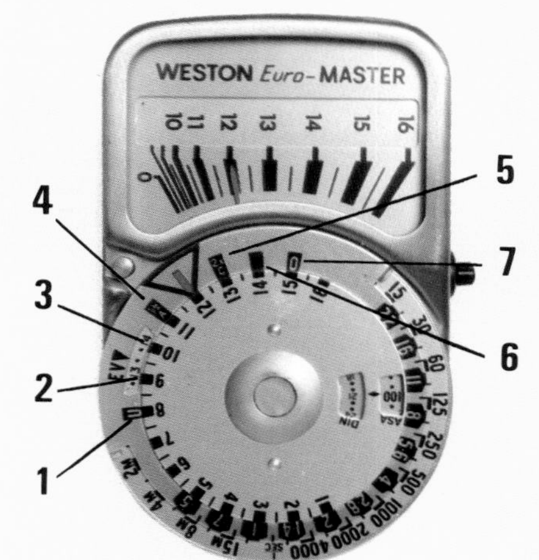

1 'U' position permits exposure determination by measurement of darkest object.

2 Provides quick means to decrease exposure by three f/stops.

3 Provides quick means to decrease exposure by two f/stops.

4 'A' position provides a means of giving half exposure.

5 'C' position provides a means of giving double exposure.

6 Provides quick means to increase exposure by two f/stops.

7 'O' position permits exposure determination by measurement of lightest object.

U & O *Using the U setting in the darkest area gives the best shadow detail, while metering from the lightest tones with the O setting concentrates on highlights*

The zone system

Fine print *By using the zone system with large format film, Ansel Adams achieved superb quality in his prints*

Of all the techniques for metering and exposure, the zone system is the most advanced—and the most complicated. Originally developed by Ansel Adams in the 1940s, it is intended mainly for black and white work, and involves preliminary darkroom work to set up the system. But once you have mastered the system, you will find that your understanding of exposure and your control of tones is much better.

The system is based on a scale of fixed tones—or *zones*—each of which is given a number (see box). By relating zones in the subject to tones which will appear in the final print, and relating both to an exposure meter reading, it is possible to finely control the range of tones in your pictures, and so get the most out of the materials. To enable you to do this, however, the processing and printing procedures must be standardized. And even the film speed may have to be altered to suit your own set-up and equipment.

First steps

Start in the darkroom to see what information a normally developed negative produces. Mark on the enlarger column a height for the enlarger which produces a convenient print size. Marking it allows you to repeat the test accurately, though you should also make extensive notes of everything that you do.

Having chosen a convenient aperture —say *f*/8—make a test strip using the unexposed edge of a negative or, better still, an unexposed frame. This means that the density of the negative is just base density plus fog. It is important, though, that the film stock and development are strictly standardized.

Make the test on grade two or three paper (whichever you use, you should use the same grade for all future prints). Give several exposures, increasing by two seconds each time, and develop fully. When dry, examine the result under a bright light. If the exposure is about right, at some point the tone steps become dense black and indistinguishable from each other. This is the deepest black of which your system is capable—zone 0. The exposure time for the first of these dense black tones is your standard printing or *standard negative exposure time*. Depending on the enlargement and your equipment it will be about ten seconds.

Having found the standard print time, you must now determine the correct film speed to use with your system, and this is done by producing a mid grey print. In effect, this calibrates your exposure meter and camera.

Set up a sheet of plain white or grey card under even illumination. Out of doors on an overcast day is ideal, provided the light level is constant. Take a reading with your usual meter at the film manufacturer's speed rating, making sure that the meter reads from the card only. Move in close if necessary, but try to standardize your procedure so that you can repeat it.

The meter will suggest an exposure which would make the card mid grey in the print, which is precisely what you want. Take a number of shots of the card at different exposures—about two stops either side of the metered reading, in half stop increments, should be sufficient. Try to keep the shutter speed constant—though it may be worth running the test several times with different shutter speeds as a check for any inaccuracies in the camera. Develop and fix using your standard procedure.

Now print the resulting negatives at the previously determined standard printing time. Compare the prints with an 18 per cent grey card and find the one which comes closest in tone. Providing you know which negative this print is made from and what exposure it had, you can determine your personal film speed, relevant to your equipment and processing. For example, if the nearest print came from the negative which was given double the metered exposure, then the true film speed should be one stop less than the recommended rating —say 64 ASA (ISO) in place of 125 ASA. This sort of adjustment is quite common with black and white film (though not so usual with colour).

At this point it is useful to make a *zone ruler*. This is a scale which shows you what the zones look like with your usual printing paper. Making such a scale involves shooting the grey card again. This time the first exposure should give four or five stops underexposure, to give zone 0 or 1 (in 35 mm photography zones 0 and 1 tend to merge due to the limited tonal range of most films). Make nine or ten exposures, giving one stop extra exposure each time. Once again it is best if you can keep the exposure time standard—preferably around 1/60 second, but in any case less than one second to avoid reciprocity failure.

Develop and print as for the other tests. The result is a series of prints from deepest black to pure white demonstrating the full range of tones. Trimmed neatly, these can serve as a reminder of the tones your equipment will produce. Of particular interest are the differences visible between zones 1, 2 and 3, and

Making a zone ruler

1 *Use a blank frame on a normally developed film. This gives you the minimum density (film base plus fog) which you will encounter in your negatives*

2 *Make a series of test prints, noting the exposure time for each. Your standard exposure time is that which produces the first maximum black*

3 *Next, take pictures of a standard grey card at the exposure suggested by a meter and bracketed exposures, marking in the frame the compensation given*

4 *Using the standard printing time, make a set of prints and find the one closest to the grey card. This shows any necessary changes to the film speed rating*

5 *Using bracketed exposures in the camera and the grey card as the subject you can make a set of prints from white to black at one stop intervals—the zone ruler*

6 *Use the zone ruler to decide what tone you want an object to be. Then meter the object and use the index mark on the dial corresponding to that zone*

Note: rendering of sky here is between zones V and VI, achieved with a yellow filter

zones 7, 8 and 9.

All of this assumes normal development in fresh developer. Even so, it sometimes happens that the zone ruler is not quite right. You might find, for example, that although zone 5 is a reasonably good match to the grey card and zone 0 (or 1) is a good deep black, zone 9 may not be pure white. This implies that the development should be increased slightly to produce a denser negative result for the highlights. This slightly alters the density of zone 5, but hardly changes the darkest zones at all.

Whenever you have a few frames left over at the end of a roll of film, use them to experiment. Try over- -and under-developing by various percentages and see what the effect is on another zone ruler series. Determine what development times enable you to keep zone 0 black, but move the higher zones up or down the brightness scale by one zone or more. Having done this, you can apply the results in the field—for example, when you need lower contrast with contrasty subjects.

Using this method to control contrast is much more accurate and predictable than any other technique—certainly much better than just guessing, which is what many photographers do. These procedures may seem complicated, but they are an important foundation, allowing you to predict what the result will be when you make the actual camera exposure.

Using the system

Compared with setting it up, using the zone system is fairly simple. You must be well acquainted with the print zones, and it is a good idea to carry the zone ruler with you, especially when you first use the system.

Zones and tones

The zone system divides the intensities of the objects in any scene into a number of bands, or *zones*, each double the brightness of the previous zone. The zones are numbered from 0 to 9 as follows:

Shadows

0 The deepest black of which the paper is capable
1 The darkest tone distinguishable from black, but without texture visible
3 Adequate texture in dark materials

Middle greys

4 Dark mid tones, such as dark leaves or shadows in portraits
5 Standard middle grey—18 per cent reflectance. Clear blue north sky
6 Light mid tone. Average white skin in sunlight or shadows in snow

Highlights

7 Very light areas, but with texture clearly visible
8 Almost white, with very little or no texture. Brightest reflections in face
9 Pure paper base white with no detail. Snow in sunlight and bright reflections in, for example, chrome

This scale represents a tonal range of 512:1 for the negative, which is reduced to about 50:1 in the print. It is possible to adapt the zone system for use with colour transparency film, but you will find it necessary to use a different set of zones. Transparency film records a tonal range of only five stops, so the zones above should be grouped in pairs (0 combined with 1, 2 with 3, and so on). You should also use a more limited range of index marks on the meter (see **page 13**).

The best approach is to use a meter which has a range of exposure index marks, such as the Weston (see page 13). These marks represent zones 1 to 8. The absence of marks for zones 0 and 9 is not a problem as these zones are simply pure black and pure white, and will rarely need to be metered for. In any case, with 35 mm photography, zones 0 and 1 often merge, as do zones 8 and 9.

The basic metering method is to first decide what zone you want a particular object tone to appear in. Say, for example, you want a flower to reproduce as zone 3. You should meter from the flower going very close if necessary to avoid metering other objects as well. Then use the mark corresponding to zone 3 as your exposure index.

The other object tones will arrange themselves according to their brightnesses relative to the flower. But you may find that the range of brightnesses is too great, or that you lose detail in another important object.

It is worth, therefore, taking readings from the brightest and darkest objects in which you want detail to appear. If both of these fall outside the normal range of zones you should either reduce development to compress the tonal range, or be prepared to sacrifice detail.

Alternatively, you may find that the range of zones is not very great. The brightness range might only be from 2 to 6, for example. In this case you could increase development slightly. But whenever you alter development, it should always be done according to previously made tests.

Another problem is that the zones might go off the scale at just one end. Putting the flower on zone three may only give you a range of zones from 0 to 5. In this case it may be wise to change the flower to zone 4 or 4½. On the other hand, such a limited tonal range is not always a problem, particularly if you actually want a low key picture (high key shots are obtained in a similar way). Although it may seem tempting to compensate for contrast problems by using different paper grades, the point of the zone system is to get the best possible negative, so that such compromises do not have to be made. Only this way can you get perfect exposures.

Using the zone system with flash

The zone system can help predict how fill-in flash will operate. Consider trying to photograph a person while the light is harsh. The meter indicates a difference of three stops between the highlight and shadow details. If the brighter parts of the face are placed on zone VI as they should be, the shadows will fall on zone III—almost featureless. If a flash gun is used to add light to the shadows a simple diagram can be drawn to show what will happen. A flash gun at normal power will give 16 units of light contribution to the scene—in other words a zone V amount.

zone No.	I	II	III	IV	V	VI	VII
equivalent units of light	1	2	4	8	16	32	64
metered subject			shadow			highlight	
add flash, 16 units			16			16	
Total resulting			20			48	

The facial highlights are now at 48 units, about zone VI½ whereas the shadows have moved proportionally more, from 4 to 20 units, ending up on zone V½. The overall exposure could be cut ½ stop to place highlights in zone VI.

Just over a stop difference between highlight and shadows may be thought too little (too much fill in) so draw another diagram to find out what will happen if a half power flash is applied. Half power equals 8 units of light.

zone No.	I	II	III	IV	V	VI	
units of light	1	2	4	8	16	32	64
metered subject			shadow			highlight	
add flash, 8 units			8			8	
Total resulting			12			40	

The difference between the two is just under two zones, about correct, and the added light would not require a decrease in exposure as between 32 and 40 units is only a quarter stop

Ansel Adams

Ansel Adams (right) is the father of the zone system. Using this system enabled him to produce pictures with stunning tonal ranges which, when combined with his undoubted creative talents, resulted in prints with great intensity and power. Original Adams prints are among the most expensive on the market, some fetching as much as a luxury car.

To get the utmost quality from his b & w film he used large format cameras, usually 5 × 4 and 10 × 8 inch. But his introduction to photography was much less auspicious.

It was in 1916, at the age of 14, that he first took up photography. His imagination was fired by the great vistas of the Yosemite Valley in California, and he attempted to record these using a box Brownie. He studied photography assiduously and quickly mastered the basic techniques. By the mid 1930s he had made his mark as a leading American photographer, highlighted by a one man exhibition at Alfred Stieglitz's gallery, *An American Place*.

The main influence on Adams was Paul Strand, and he collaborated with people like Edward Weston, who all shared a love of the 'fine print'. Two of his most important photographs—*Banner Peak* (1923) and *The Half Dome* (1926)—were steps on the way to realizing that the photographic medium is a craft which needs to be carefully controlled and understood. To this end he developed the zone system—a method which demands that the photographer be aware of the precise effects of exposure and development.

The zone system has been known to inspire almost fanatical devotion in some of its most ardent followers, who tend to rate technical quality above aspects such as interesting subject matter, or good composition. Nevertheless the zone system remains, forty years on, the standard technique for ultimate b & w print quality.

Advanced focusing

Inaccurate focusing probably spoils more photographs than any other technical fault. Most modern cameras automatically set the correct exposure, but usually leave the user to set the focus. This is usually relatively straightforward. However, there are occasions when the conditions or the subject make focusing difficult.

There may be times when you do not wish to make your presence obvious, such as in candid street photography. For such occasions you need a focusing method which enables you to produce a sharp image without drawing attention to the camera by holding it up to your eye and focusing it in the normal way. You may also have to deal with a rapidly moving subject, in which case you will not have time to set the focus. In low light, you may not be able even to see the subject clearly enough to focus properly. At other times, the subject itself may be the problem—its surface texture may defeat the camera's focusing aids, or it may extend beyond the depth of field of the lens you are using. While focusing in such situations is more difficult than usual, there are several techniques you can use to make it easier.

Fast focusing

Parties and street scenes are typical situations where the rapid and irregular movement of the subject can make focusing a hit-or-miss business. Indoors, low light aggravates this, and asking people to stop for the camera destroys the spontaneity of the situation.

If you are using a camera with interchangeable lenses, you can make fast focusing easier by fitting a wide angle lens. This gives you greater depth of field, so that more will be in focus, and also has the advantage that the focusing ring usually rotates through a relatively small arc, making focusing quicker. If you use high speed film with such a lens you can choose a small aperture, thus increasing your depth of field so that almost everything will be in focus.

At parties or similar gatherings, a portable flashgun fitted to your camera can allow you to set a small aperture on your normal or wide angle lens so that you need not worry about focusing at all —you just have to make sure that your subject is within the depth of field of the lens and within the range of the flash gun. If you have an automatic electronic flash, set the lens aperture to match the aperture indicated on the flash calculator dial. Usually the dial indicates a maximum distance at which the flash can be used. If your lens has a depth of field scale, set this distance on the focusing ring opposite the mark on the scale for the aperture you have set. This technique will give you maximum depth of field, allowing you to take photographs at a range of distances knowing that as much as possible will appear sharp.

Take care when using a wide angle lens and a flashgun together—you may need to fit a diffuser panel to the flash head to increase the illumination coverage to light the subject fully.

Zone focusing

For candid photography and for other occasions when you do not want to use flash, there are other ways of ensuring that the subject is kept in focus. When there is insufficient time to focus through the viewfinder in the regular way you can try adopting the method used by some manufacturers of rangefinder cameras, known as zone focusing. Instead of precise distances in feet and metres, symbols are marked on the focusing ring—a head for the close-up setting, a group of figures for the middle distance and a mountain for the infinity setting. When the lens is set for a given zone,

Girl on swing *With moving subjects, preset the point of sharp focus, and shoot when your subject reaches it*

Zone 1 *Focused on 1.1 metres*

Zone 2 *Focused on 1.75 metres*

Zone 3 *Focused on 3 metres*

Front of queue *With the lens focused on 1.1 m, only the stallholder and the first customer are in focus*

Middle of queue *The second zone of sharp focus includes only the next of the figures in the queue*

Back of queue *With the lens set to the green mark, the first two figures are unsharp, and the rest are in focus*

Zone focusing *By using preset zones it is possible to make snap judgements about where to set the focusing ring without having to lift the camera conspicuously up to your eye*

all objects within the zone are sharp. Of course this system works better if you are able to benefit from the broad depth of field of a wide angle lens or a small aperture. Focusing becomes very much more difficult to accomplish with this method if a lens longer than 50 or 55 mm is used or if a normal lens is used at full aperture.

If you have a rough idea of how far away your subjects are likely to be, you can identify these distances on the focusing ring so that you can rapidly preset the focus before you raise the camera to your eye. To accomplish this, some photographers use the night photography technique described on page 51. Tape small pieces of matchstick to specific focus positions—in this case, for example, one match might indicate what is likely to be the closest distance to be used on your lens's focusing scale. This is followed by two pieces side by side at a middle distance, and three pieces at a farther distance. Rotating the focusing ring until the appropriate zone is at the 12 o'clock position and aligning the matchsticks with the index mark on the focusing scale by touch, you can set an estimated distance without even looking at your focusing scale.

All this presupposes that you are reasonably familiar with the controls of your camera so that you can handle it literally with your eyes closed. It also assumes that you can make a reasonably good estimate of the distance to your subject. This sort of ability is the result of practice. An hour or so of guessing distances and then checking them against the distances given by the focusing aids in your camera is usually enough to improve your ability considerably.

For candid shots outdoors, there are other methods often practised by photographers who specialize in catching people unawares. One method is to focus on another subject a similar distance away, then turn the camera on to the subject you are really interested in and quickly press the shutter. With a wide angle lens, you can even include people in the frame without them knowing it. They will think you are shooting past them and are unlikely to realize how much your camera is taking in. Another method involves anticipating where your subject is likely to walk into view. By prefocusing on a point on the ground and waiting for the subject to walk past that particular spot, you can take a photograph very quickly by just raising the camera to your eye at the last possible moment.

Fast moving subjects

Cars, trains, aircraft and other fast moving subjects present special focusing problems. Sometimes the subject may be moving across your field of view at an angle or at a considerable distance, and you have to successfully adjust the focus continuously to keep the subject sharp. This technique is known as follow focusing but can only be employed effectively if the subject is at a reasonable distance away. To make follow focusing easier, Novoflex manufacture a range of telephoto lenses with pistol grips to control the focus. Squeezing the control focuses the lens progressively closer, and relaxing it allows the focus to return towards infinity.

However, if the subject is close or moving more or less directly towards or away from you, you may have to preset the focus, just as for walking subjects. Find a point on the ground that the subject can be expected to pass over and focus on this. When the subject reaches this point it will be in focus.

Focusing markers *Certain cameras have quick focus rings fitted with movable markers to indicate focus zones*

There is a slight complication, though—if you wait until the subject is in focus before you release the shutter, the brief time delay between pressing the shutter release button and the operation of the shutter mechanism may be enough to let the subject pass out of focus, especically if it is moving quickly. This delay is known as time parallax, and it varies in duration from camera to camera. In general SLRs have greater time parallax than rangefinder cameras since their viewing mirrors have to be raised before the shutter can operate.

The solution to the problem is to release the shutter slightly before the subject reaches the focused point. If, for instance, the subject is a racing car, you may well decide that the driver's cockpit is the most desirable position to have in focus. But if the car is coming towards you at speed, you will need to press the shutter at the moment when the nose of the car crosses the point of prefocus. This will allow for the time parallax so that the cockpit will be crossing the focusing point at the time the actual exposure is made. Consistent success can only be achieved if you practise this technique and learn from your mistakes.

Parallax focusing

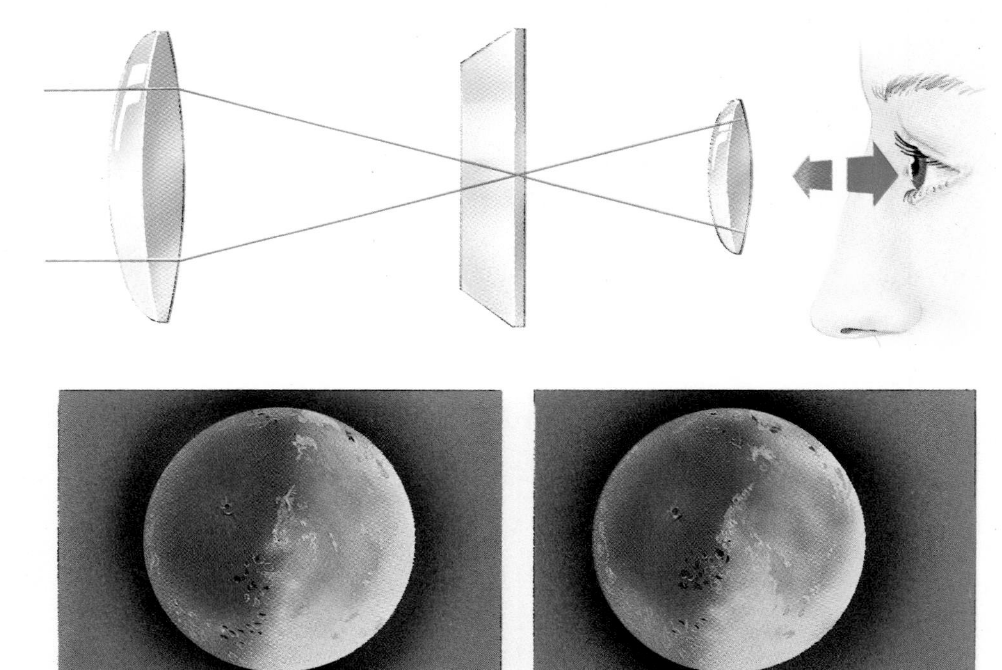

Using clear screens *In certain conditions, it may be impossible to use a matt glass screen, and instead a clear screen with cross hairs is used. When the image of the subject is in focus, it does not move in relation to the screen if the photographer's head is rocked gently to and fro*

Split image screens

The focusing aids built in to SLRs can cope with most situations. However, there are some subjects that are difficult to deal with even with the combined help of split image rangefinders, microprisms and glass focusing screens.

Cats and rabbits, for example, are often physically uncooperative—they tend not to sit still when you want them to—and their fur is difficult to focus on yet must be really sharp to be effective in a photograph. Fur is impossible to focus with split image rangefinder prisms unless it has a strong pattern. Microprisms are somewhat more effective but can be misleading when you are dealing with long-furred animals at close ranges. Try to focus on the centre of the animal rather than its outline. If you are shooting a portrait of your pet, try to focus on the eyes, just as when you photograph a person.

Some subjects can mislead your focusing system. Split image rangefinders are usually effective with subjects having strong horizontal or vertical lines on their surface, but not when the lines form a regular pattern as with striped wallpaper. In such cases you may find that you have matched the wrong lines of the pattern, giving an image that looks satisfactory in the split image prisms yet is out of focus. With such subjects you should always check your focusing on the matt glass area of your focusing screen.

One difficulty widely experienced with focusing is that one half of a split image screen may black out. This only happens with lenses of a relatively small maximum aperture. But this itself is particularly irritating since lenses with smaller apertures tend to be of longer focal lengths and require more critical focusing techniques. In some cases you will find that this difficulty can be overcome by placing your eye closer to the viewfinder or by using a rubber eyecup. However, often there is no way of improving matters and one of the other focusing aids has to be used. Usually a camera which offers a split image screen also allows focusing to be accomplished by microprisms or by the plain matt glass area of the screen. Cameras with

Adding light *Sometimes, you may need a light to focus by. Remove it to take the actual photograph*

interchangeable screens can be fitted with the appropriate screen which will make focusing much easier for certain subjects.

Using a tape measure

There are occasions when the easiest way to overcome focusing problems is to measure the distance from the camera to the subject with a tape measure. Dark subjects, for instance, can be particularly tricky to deal with. However, in such cases you can try to bracket the focusing by taking several exposures with the focusing ring moved slightly between shots.

If your subject is close and stationary you may find it easier to measure the distance and to set this distance on your focusing ring.

To make certain that this is done accurately, the distance should be measured from the most important part of your subject to the film plane. The location of the film plane is indicated by a mark which is usually scribed on the top plate of the camera.

Fast focusing *Novoflex lenses have an ingenious squeeze-to-focus action that makes follow focus techniques easier*

Where possible, a simple solution to focusing on dark subjects is to shine more light on to the subject while you focus. After focusing, the extra light can be removed or extinguished while the exposure is made. Additional light can be supplied by a mirror, domestic lights or a torch.

Autofocus problems

There are two main types of autofocus systems—known as active and passive. Both are likely to make mistakes under some circumstances. Active systems work by emitting a pulse of light or sound and computing the distance to the subject either by measuring the angle at which the pulse is reflected, or in the case of the Polaroid Sonar system, the length of time taken for the pulse to return to the camera.

In either case, if the subject does not act as a suitable reflecting surface for the pulse from the camera, results may be unsatisfactory. With the Sonar system, some hard surfaces at an angle to the line of sight can reflect the sound pulses away from the camera altogether, leading the camera to set focus at infinity. The only practical way to avoid these problems is to make sure that there are no steeply angled surfaces within your field of view, and that you do not exceed the close focusing limit of your camera.

Passive autofocus systems are just as prone to error. Most work by detecting subject contrast, although mechanical details may vary. All need light to operate, and some may not be able to focus in light levels that are still bright enough for ordinary photography. Flat, even surfaces without much subject detail usually defeat contrast measuring systems. Some systems are sensitive to the angle of lines on the subject, and may work better when held vertically rather than horizontally.

Both active and passive systems are often fooled by intervening objects such as foliage, bars or panes of glass. Fortunately, most autofocus systems can be manually overridden.

Chapter 2

HANDLING DAYLIGHT

Coping with contrast

In the early days of the camera, photographers would often wait for the sun to come out before shooting and, even today, a bright sunny day seems the ideal time for taking pictures. Unfortunately, too much light can often create just as many problems as too little light.

In strong sunshine, the difference in brightness between the brightest highlights and the deepest shadows—the contrast range—may be so extreme that even the most versatile modern film cannot cope. The photographer must therefore expose either for the highlights or the shadows. If you expose for the highlights, detail in the shadows will be lost: if you expose for the shadows, highlight detail and colour may be lost. This can be particularly unpleasant with portraits, where one side of the face is properly illuminated but the other is in deep shadow. Strong sunshine also throws harsh shadows over the subject.

You can, of course, wait for the sun to go behind a cloud or move your subject into the shadow. A better solution is to illuminate or 'fill in' the shadows.

The easiest and cheapest way to add fill-in light is to use reflectors. You can buy specially made reflectors in a range of sizes, but virtually any light coloured surface can act as a reflector. You probably have several potential reflectors in your home. Sheets of white card or paper, mirrors, kitchen foil stuck to boards, even sheets and towels are all suitable. But do not restrict yourself only to portable reflectors. Look for natural reflectors in the landscape such as bright sand or whitewashed walls.

To be effective, a reflector must catch

Fence sitter ***A high contrast range need not cause problems if you take your exposure reading from the main subject***

Portrait ***Exposure has been set to give normal tones on the face, while the background has been made much less obtrusive by underexposure***

Reduced contrast *The overall contrast range of the subject can be reduced if a reflector is used to throw light into the shadows. This gives a more pleasing result*

Sunlight contrast *The bright light of the sun can be too strong for many subjects. Harsh shadows may result, particularly when colour slide film is used*

light from the sun and reflect it into the shadows on the subject. This means that it has to face the light and point towards the subject. Remembering that light is reflected from a surface at the same angle at which it hits the surface, you can work out theoretically the ideal position and angle for your reflector. In practice, though, it is much simpler to set up fill-in reflectors by eye. Adjust the angle and tilt of the reflector until you get the effect you want. If you have a friend with you, ask him or her to hold the reflector and aim it at the subject while you look through the viewfinder. Make sure that the reflector itself is not visible at the edge of the viewfinder. When you are working on your own, this may call for

Placing a reflector *In bright sunshine, a small white board can be used as a reflector. Prop it in a suitable position facing the shadows*

more careful adjustment of the reflector position. Rigid reflectors can usually be leaned against some firm support, while flexible reflectors such as sheets or towels can be taped to or stretched over a suitable support.

You can check the brightness range of the subject with a light meter (see page 8-9) but it is quicker to estimate the effects with your eyes. But remember that your eyes can see more than the camera, so always add slightly more fill-in light than appears to be necessary.

Reflectors are invaluable in many situations. With backlit shots, for instance, all detail may be lost unless you properly illuminate the front of the subject. Use a reflector approximately at the camera position to throw light back onto the subject. With subjects lit strongly from the side, place a reflector on the opposite side of the subjects from the sun.

Fill-in flash

Using a flash gun to brighten the shadows is another way to control contrast outdoors. It does not matter whether the flash is a manual or automatic unit, although there are differences in the techniques involved for each type.

When you use fill-in flash always remember that the object is not to use flash as the main light source. Outdoors this would produce an unnatural effect, and in any case would require a very powerful flash gun with most normal SLR cameras. You should always give less exposure when using a flash gun as a fill-in than you would when using it as a main light source. As a rule of thumb for most subjects, work out the exposure you would use if you were using flash as the main light, and then close down the aperture one stop.

Procedure

First set your camera to the correct shutter speed to synchronize with flash. With most cameras with focal plane shutters this is 1/60, but some focal plane shutters synchronize at up to 1/250, and between the lens shutters synchronize at all shutter speeds. Refer to your camera's instruction book for guidance.

Next take a light reading of the general scene and set the aperture the meter recommends to suit the flash synchronization speed.

If you are using a manual flash gun, the distance from the flash to the subject

Flash outdoors *As an alternative to reflectors, use a portable, electronic camera-mounted flash to balance the subject shadows with the highlights*

Balancing flash and daylight *Exposing for the scene outside gives a main subject that is too dark. Exposing for the subject would wash out the exterior*

affects the exposure given by the gun. However, since the exposure that you set on your camera is determined by the amount of light falling on the subject from the sun, there is normally only a limited choice of apertures, and hence flash to subject distances available. For example, if you have loaded Kodachrome 25 into your camera your exposure in bright sunlight would typically need to be about 1/60 at *f*/11. Your flash gun would need to be positioned at the correct distance for making an exposure with the aperture set one stop wider, at *f*/8. If you have a close-focusing zoom lens, you can mount the flash gun on the camera and move both camera and flash to the appropriate distance. Then you can reframe the picture with the zoom control. The alternative is to put the flash gun on a long sync lead so that you can adjust the distance of the flash gun without moving the camera.

With an automatic flash gun your distance from the subject may be varied up to the maximum distance given by the flash at that particular aperture. For example, with your camera set at 1/60 at *f*/11, you should set the flash gun so that it would give correct exposure if the lens were set at *f*/8. Not all automatic flash guns allow you to choose your aperture settings in this way; if yours does not, set the gun on manual.

In order to produce enough light to be used for fill-in flash at distances suitable for full-length portraits, a fairly powerful flash gun is necessary. This is not surprising, if you think about how the exposure is made up. A small electronic flash gun delivers all its output in no more than 1/500 sec. Yet the construction of focal plane shutters means that the powerful light of the sun has 1/60 sec to affect the film, and the aperture must be set to match this. Therefore you must move in close to your subject, to make the most of the power you have, or use a more powerful flash gun than most amateur units, or use a camera with a between the lens shutter so you can set a faster shutter and a wider aperture.

Moving in closer is the simplest answer, but may create problems with composition and framing. Fitting a wide angle lens can help, but only if your flash produces a broad enough beam to cover the view angle of the lens. Nevertheless, since many scenes where you want to use fill-in flash have a central subject with a brightly lit background, your flash gun need not have such wide coverage as would be necessary in more routine uses.

Buying a more powerful flash gun is a worthwhile course of action if you use fill-in flash often. The main disadvantages are the cost and weight of really powerful flash units. Automatic flash guns powerful enough to give you plenty of distance between you and your subject are usually large units with separate power packs.

Professional photographers often buy roll film SLRs with between the lens shutters because they synchronize with electronic flash at all speeds, in addition to their other advantages. This too is an expensive way of making fill-in flash pictures, but you need not go quite so far. Most compact rangefinder cameras have between the lens shutters that synchronize at all speeds, although sometimes their instruction books are not completely clear about how they may be used with this technique. If you have a compact rangefinder camera, experiment with a roll of colour slide film at various combinations of aperture, shutter speed and (with automatic flash guns) flash output to find a setting that gives you the results you want. You are likely to find that a compact camera, which you may have as a 'second' camera, is more suitable for this sort of work than a more expensive SLR.

Fill-in flash experiments

Fill-in flash is a technique that lends itself to a large number of variations. Most experiments are made much easier by using an automatic flash gun, but a manual flash gun can be used.

The first variable you can alter is the ratio between the fill-in flash and the natural light. Setting a lens aperture one stop smaller than that indicated by the flash calculator dial provides a level of fill lighting that may be stronger than you need. For a less obtrusive effect, try setting an aperture another stop smaller than that indicated by the flash calculator.

The opposite approach is to make the electronic flash the main source of light in your picture, and use the natural light for fill. Since this means using a sufficiently high flash output to overpower the

Adding flash *With a focal plane shutter, you may be forced to use a relatively slow shutter speed. This can cause overexposure of exterior scenes*

Balanced light levels *A between the lens shutter allows you to set a higher shutter speed to control the effect of existing light. Interior and exterior are correct*

natural light, the natural light must be relatively dim. In late evening or on very cloudy days you may be able to achieve these conditions. Simply set the lens aperture to the setting indicated by the flash dial and work in the normal way.

A technique that has been used to good effect by fashion and creative photographers is to use flash combined with a long shutter speed. In low light this produces an interesting blur effect in the background of your photograph, while the foreground subject lit primarily by flash remains sharp. Since the subject is lit twice, by both natural light and flash, you must close the lens down a stop smaller than the indicated meter reading to avoid overexposure, and use this aperture as the basis for your flash setting. Use a slow film so that you can set a sufficiently slow shutter speed to produce a blur effect.

Other effects involving the use of gelatin filters, taped over the flash tube, are possible. Try taping an 85B, which balances tungsten film to daylight, over the flash tube and loading tungsten film into your camera. In daylight, subjects within the range of the flash are reproduced with approximately their normal colours, while the rest of the picture becomes a pronounced twilight blue. Other possible combinations can be found by experiment.

Fashion shot *An 85C warming filter was taped over the flash tube to fill in shadow detail without affecting the colour balance and mood of the picture*

Shots against the light

You still sometimes hear people reminding photographers that they have not got the sun behind them. At one time, when snapshot cameras and lenses were very limited, this was a necessary precaution for successful pictures. But thanks to mass production and lens multicoating, even quite cheap cameras can take bright sparkling pictures in which the sun, or another light source, appears. Nevertheless, photographers still hesitate before pointing their cameras towards a bright light. Those that do rarely regret it, because *contre jour* lighting can be the making of a picture.

Taking pictures into the light, though, is not as straightforward as photographing with the light behind you. Exposure meters are easily misled by the high contrasts, and extra care must be taken to avoid flare. On the other hand, provided you understand what the problems are, and how to overcome them, you should not find it difficult to photograph even when the light shines directly into the lens.

How to avoid flare

The main problem in photographing a bright light source is that the brilliant rays of light have to pass through several layers of glass, with air gaps in between them, and past various metal and plastic surfaces, before finally reaching the film. Reflections and light scattering can take place anywhere along the way, and any part of the scattered light that eventually reaches the film no longer forms a focused image of the subject, but instead causes flare.

The most noticeable form of flare is that which results from strong reflections from one or two surfaces only. This kind of flare forms a strong flare spot or patch on the film, often in the shape of the diaphragm opening. It is also possible to see ghost images of the light source itself, on the opposite side of the frame.

The other form of flare is less immediately obvious. This is general flare over the whole image area which effectively gives a low level fogging exposure to the film. The main effect of this type of flare is a reduction in contrast and brilliance. On colour film it reduces colour saturation, and imparts a misty, veiled atmosphere to the scene.

Further trouble from flare can arise even when powerful light rays have left the rear elements of the lens. Reflections can occur on the film, too, and these take two forms. First there is *halation* which is caused by light passing through the emulsion, striking the film base and being reflected back into the emulsion to form a secondary image. Since the reflected rays do not follow the same path as the original ray, the image spreads out. Modern films have very efficient antihalation bases, though, and this particular effect is only visible when very bright light sources appear in the picture.

The other effect within the film is a form of diffusion. Light rays striking the silver halide grains are reflected on to other grains not directly illuminated. Again the result is spreading out of the image so that bright highlights are not

Black car *One or two stops extra exposure is needed if a light source is visible—a TTL meter is easily misled*

Sunlit silhouette *(left) Exposing for the sky and sun reduces subjects in shadow to a stark black outline*

sharp and hard edged on the film, but rather blurred and soft.

In most cases where a photographer points a camera into the light, elimination of flare is of paramount importance. The antireflection coating on modern lenses helps in this respect, but there are other precautions which you can take to cut flare even further.

The first of these is to use as uncomplicated a lens as you can while retaining quality. Since light scattering takes place at each air–glass interface, the fewer of these there are, the less of a problem flare is likely to be. Zoom lens designs, by their very nature, are complicated, so never use a zoom lens for shooting into the light if you can avoid it—unless you are deliberately trying to emphasize flare for creative reasons. Standard lenses are usually comparatively flare free, as are the majority of good quality telephoto lenses. Wide angles, particularly recent designs, are quite complex, and are prone to flare.

One of the simplest precautions that you can take to minimize flare is to make sure that you have a clean lens. Although overfrequent and vigorous lens cleaning can lead to scratching of the lens surfaces, occasional careful cleaning causes no damage, and is a necessity for flare free pictures.

Do not just wipe the front element with a handkerchief or shirt tail, but remove dust and grit methodically. First remove any surface dirt with a soft brush. This prevents grit from being ground into the glass when the lens is wiped. If the glass is still dirty, take an ordinary paper handkerchief, fold it in half four times, then tear the folded wad into two. Use the torn ends to clean the lens, wiping marks off in a circular motion, starting in the centre and working outwards. Finally, remove any fluff with a brush.

Really stubborn marks, such as greasy fingerprints, can be removed by breathing gently on the lens, then wiping with a tissue. Remember to clean the rear element of the lens, too.

Flare is encouraged by using a filter or any other front-of-lens accessory except a lens hood. If you normally use a skylight filter to protect your lens, remove this when shooting into the light. If you really must use a filter for some reason, use the best quality you can find, preferably a glass filter that is antireflection coated. Avoid using plastic filters—these are never coated—and never use more than one filter at a time.

The aperture to which the lens is set

Reflected glow *Deliberate underexposure can make a good picture from a dull subject*

Roadside view *Backlighting can cause flare that softens the image, and cuts down contrast*

Sometimes, particularly when photographing a sunset in which the sun is quite bright, a ghost image of the sun appears in a particularly undesirable part of the picture. It may be possible to deal with this by altering the composition so that the ghost image coincides with another bright part of the picture, such as a reflection on water. Alternatively, you may find that all you can do is to place the sun at the centre of the picture, so that its ghost image coincides with its real image. This sometimes produces a ring of light centred on the sun, however.

Getting the exposure right

When a light source appears in a picture, the tonal range of the scene—the subject contrast—becomes many times higher than usual. The sun, for example, is 100,000 times brighter than the most brilliant highlight in the scene it illuminates.

This exposure range is far greater than any film can handle, and the inevitable result is that the light source, when it appears in a picture, is overexposed. What you as the photographer must decide, though, is how much overexposure of the light source is acceptable. This varies from picture to picture, according to how much detail is required in the other parts of the photograph. If you are taking a backlit portrait, for example, in which the sun appears over the shoulder of the model, detail in the sitter's face is important, so exposing for the sun is out of the question. On the other hand, in a street scene at night, the light sources themselves and their immediate surroundings—the street lights, car headlights and brightly lit

Headlight trails *To prevent flare in night pictures, carefully clean your lens, and avoid the use of a zoom*

Music lesson *Fill-in flash helps to put light into the shadows when the main light is behind the subject*

also has an effect on flare. At a wide aperture, marginal rays entering the lens are more likely to strike the edges of the lens elements, causing the light to scatter. Even stopping a lens down half a stop from its maximum aperture can eliminate this source of flare. On the other hand, once the lens is stopped down to a very small aperture flare again begins to increase, because light is scattered by the blades of the diaphragm.

Some flare patterns can be subtle, and may not be noticeable on the camera's viewing screen, which has rather low contrast. When you see the result, however, you may find that the flare is now only too obvious, thanks to the higher contrast of slide film in particular. One way to check for such hidden flare is to move the camera slightly, so that the flare pattern will change its position. This may make it easier to spot, and you may be able to avoid it altogether by stopping down further.

windows—may be the only parts of the subject that are bright enough to appear on film. Here, shadow detail usually disappears completely, so overexposure of the light sources is not so acceptable—they make up the principal subject.

Each individual case must be judged on its own merits. Think carefully about which part of the picture constitutes the main point of interest—are you trying to take a photograph of the light source itself, or is the area that it illuminates more important? The TTL meter in a camera generally indicates an exposure which records a plain subject as an even mid tone on the film. To measure the exposure, then, you must first decide which part of the subject is to appear as a mid tone, and take a selective meter reading from that part.

In the case of the backlit portrait, mentioned above, the model's face is the area which is to appear as a mid tone. Though this is in shadow, it is the area from which you must take a meter reading. The sun is still included in the picture but in this case, it forms a burned out area of overexposure.

For the night scene, the situation is different. Here, the important parts of the picture are the light sources and the areas around them, so your meter reading should concentrate on these parts of the picture and not on the shadows. A reading taken from the roof of a car parked under a street lamp should suggest an appropriate exposure.

If you have an automatic camera, *key tone* readings like this may be quite difficult. If possible, use the camera manually, or use the memory lock button if your camera is fitted with one. A straight reading taken in the normal way will almost certainly lead to under-exposure when a bright light source is in the picture, unless it is balanced by an equivalent amount of deep shadow, so if you have neither manual control nor a memory lock, you may be able to get the correct exposure by using the backlight button or exposure compensation dial, which should be set to ×4, or +2. Alternatively, reset the ASA dial to a lower film speed—this will also result in extra exposure. As a further precaution against incorrect exposure, try and bracket your pictures if you can, by making exposures at one stop above and below that recommended by the meter.

The problems that crop up when a light source appears in the picture are very similar to those encountered when lighting comes from behind the subject or from one side. The harsh contrast that this sort of lighting generates can be reduced by using fill-in flash, or a reflector to put light into the shadows.

Using flare creatively

It is not always necessary to totally eliminate flare, and sometimes it can be used to brighten up a dull picture. The two different types of flare—general veiling flare and octagonal diaphragm

Sun and flowers ***Octagonal flare spots need not spoil your picture. In this image they echo the drops on the leaves***

spots can be generated in different ways, and each gives quite a different kind of feel to the picture. Veiling flare conjures up a misty, romantic mood, but brightly coloured flare spots give an impression of dynamism, and a modern, active look.

Veiling flare is only too easy to produce. Pastel and soft focus filters rely on it for their effect, but there are simpler, cheaper ways of introducing it. Lining a lens hood with crumpled metal foil is a sure way of doing this—pieces of gauze or crumpled cellophane partly covering the lens are equally effective. Try breathing on the lens in cold weather. Though this requires no extra equipment, it is rather unpredictable. Using a zoom lens at full aperture is a sure way of generating flare when the light source is visible in the picture.

Flare spots are slightly more difficult to control. Set the lens to its minimum aperture, and press the stopdown button on your camera. If you then point the camera at the light source, flare patterns are usually clearly visible, but their position in the frame depends on that of the light source itself. Getting the string of colourful octagons where you want it may not be as easy as it seems. They show up best where they cross an area of shadow, and can be almost invisible on highlight areas.

High key, low key

In most photographs, there is an even range of tones from dark to light—any picture that shows a dearth of dark or light tones is generally under- or over-exposed. But by deliberately tipping the balance towards dark tones, you can produce a rich, moody *low key* picture. By keeping tones predominantly light, on the other hand, you can create a cool, delicate *high key* effect. To get the best from both high and low key shots, though, you must choose your subject carefully and use special lighting techniques.

For an effective high key shot, you must choose a subject that is very light in colour: for a low key shot, the subject must be dark. But the lighting must enhance these qualities. High key lighting is very flat and soft, with few shadows, whereas low key lighting is selective, and only the principal area of interest is brightly lit.

Traditionally, black and white film has been used for high and low key photographs, because it offers the photographer more control over the tonal range and contrast of the final image. Nevertheless, high and low key images can be equally effective in colour. For high key work in colour, you must be careful in your selection of subject matter, because the high levels of lighting show up every slight difference in colour. Essentially, high key shots should have only one or two main colours—white is particularly suitable. Low key lighting, however, tends to disguise colour differences, and looks effective in colour.

High key treatment

High key effects can only be achieved with subjects that are predominantly light in tone—small patches of darker tone, such as dark eyes on a nude, do not matter too much, and may prevent a high key picture looking pale and insipid.

Popular subjects for high key shots are nudes and portraits, particularly where the sitter has blonde or light coloured hair, but still lifes can be equally effective. Room interiors also work well if they are very pale and sufficiently brightly and evenly lit.

Out of doors, high key pictures are much more difficult to take because there is less control over the lighting and subject matter, but it is possible to produce effective landscapes under the right conditions. A fall of snow, for instance, can obliterate most dark tones from a landscape, and provide an ideal opportunity for high key pictures. Sand dunes and desert scenery also have possibilities.

Avoid any subject, indoors or out, that has large areas of dark tones. This more or less rules out dark-haired models, or at least makes the posing of them very difficult.

It is sometimes possible to conceal areas of dark tone by using *diffusion filters* on the lens to soften the focus. Because these spill light from the highlights into the shadows, they emphasize the high key effect, and work particularly well with figure studios and misty, romantic portraits.

Backgrounds for high key studio pictures must be similarly light toned. Seamless white paper makes an excellent background, providing there is enough space between the main subject and the background to light the background separately and eliminate shadows.

Winter whiteness ***Cold weather is ideal for high key pictures. Obtrusive dark areas are blanketed by snow and ice, so it is an easy matter to shoot high key pictures out of doors. Best results are produced in overcast weather, where the shadows are soft and subdued—this is an important element of a high key treatment. Nevertheless, you can achieve a good high key effect even in bright sunshine providing you avoid including any strong colours in the frame—the pale blue of the winter sky is as much as you can get away with. Work on north facing slopes to keep snow in shade.***

Dark landscape *The subdued colours and dark skies that you sometimes see after a storm provide a perfect opportunity for low key landscape pictures*

Low key look *A low key treatment works well for people with black skin, but it is essential to use a hard light source to put in bright highlights*

Alternatively, work in a room with white walls and, ideally, white or near-white floor coverings. Dark-coloured fitted carpets, or a dark wood floor can easily be covered with a white painted hardboard sheet. Try to keep all the props for the picture pale in colour too.

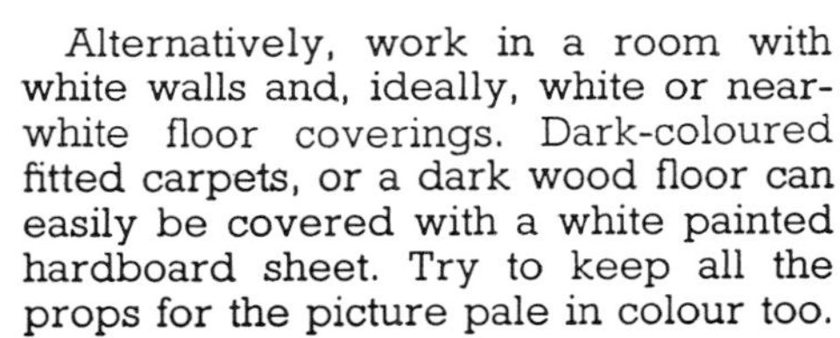

Setting up the shot

With the subject chosen and a suitable background arranged, you must carefully light both subject and background to emphasize their pale colour. The idea is to eliminate virtually all shadow from the picture, leaving just enough to give an impression of shape and form.

Place the subject well away from the background and position the key light—the main light source—quite close to the camera, at about 30° to the lens axis. This keeps the shadow areas smaller than they are when the light is farther out to one side. The key light can be quite small, and a photoflood bulb in a 20 cm reflector is perfectly adequate.

The next stage is to use a second, much softer light source to fill in the shadows created by the key light and give the short tonal range characteristic of high key pictures.

This fill-in light must provide much more gentle, even illumination than the key light. A large matt-white reflector with a cap to cover the bulb is ideal, but there are other ways of softening the beam from a tungsten lamp. One way is to use a normal small reflector, and bounce the light from a large sheet of polystyrene or white card. Another alternative is to stretch two layers of tracing paper (or specially made diffusion material) over a wooden frame, and use this in front of the light to diffuse its beam. Either of these techniques produces the soft, flat lighting that is needed, even from quite a small light source.

Move this second light source around until the shadows from the key light are just visible. But avoid moving the second light so close that it creates its own shadows.

Finally, light the background to bring it up to approximately the same level of brightness as the main subject. You may be able to do this using only one light, placing it in front of the background and above it, just outside the picture area—if the background is very large, though, two lamps are needed, one at each side.

The level of light for the background should be either slightly darker, or slightly paler than the main subject. If both subject and background are exactly the same brightness, the two will merge together, and the contours of the subject will be lost. Use an exposure meter, and check that there is a small difference in brightness between the subject and its background.

Proper exposure is essential for high key work but it can be difficult to achieve, because a normal reading with a TTL meter would lead to under exposure. Since the subject is pale in colour and reflects a great deal of light, a reflected light reading would indicate too little exposure.

For correct exposure, an *incident light* reading is essential—that is, a reading for the light falling on the subject. This should ideally be made with a hand-held meter with a plastic diffuser dome in place. To take the reading, stand directly in front of the subject and point the meter at the camera. If you do not have a separate meter, and rely on the TTL meter in your camera, use an 18 per cent grey card, and take a reflected light reading from this. You should get the same result as you would from an incident light meter.

Whichever method of metering you use, it is a sensible precaution to bracket the pictures—in addition to the indicated exposure, make exposures at half stop intervals for two stops either side. This way, you have a number of negatives or transparencies with slightly different densities from which to choose. If you are using black and white film, bracket at one stop intervals.

The film should be processed in exactly the same way as usual. Do not be alarmed by the appearance of the film as it comes out of the developing tank—negatives look very dense, and slides seem to be overexposed. This is what constitutes a high key picture, and as soon as you examine the images carefully, you will see that all the detail has been retained.

Low key pictures

Low key pictures need a generally dark toned subject, but if there are any pale areas in the subject or background they can often be concealed in shadow. The range of subjects suitable for low key treatment is therefore greater than that for high key pictures. In particular, it is relatively easy to achieve a low key effect out of doors, particularly when there is plenty of dark foliage in the picture.

However, before you aim for a low key image, make sure that it will suit the subject—it is easy to produce low key pictures that are inappropriately sombre and funereal, and have rather a depressing air. Only use a low key treatment if the subject is sufficiently full of life to override this, or if you are deliberately trying to conjure up a forbidding mood.

A low key picture is more difficult to light than a high key one, because the approach must be varied to suit the subject. Ideally, there should only be a small bright highlight—usually on the main part of the subject—and detail should be just visible in the shadows. Shape and form should be just suggested and hinted at, rather than being emphatically stated.

Where texture needs to be emphasized—with fabrics, for instance, or a wrinkled face—a small hard light source should be positioned to bring out surface detail. If texture is to be subdued, softer lighting may be more suitable, and light should be placed closer to the camera. In both cases, though, lamps should be shielded so that light does not spill into areas which are to remain in shadow.

The main source of light is used to create the highlight, but the rest of the picture needs to be lit by a very low intensity light source. This should just be bright enough to produce detail on the negative, or to lift the dark

Low key lunch *The lighting for this still life was very simple. The photographer used only one light source, a sheet of tracing paper lit from behind by two powerful floodlights. The rich shadows that are a characteristic of low key lighting were created by shading the set using large pieces of black card. The centre of the picture was left unshaded and is much more brightly illuminated*

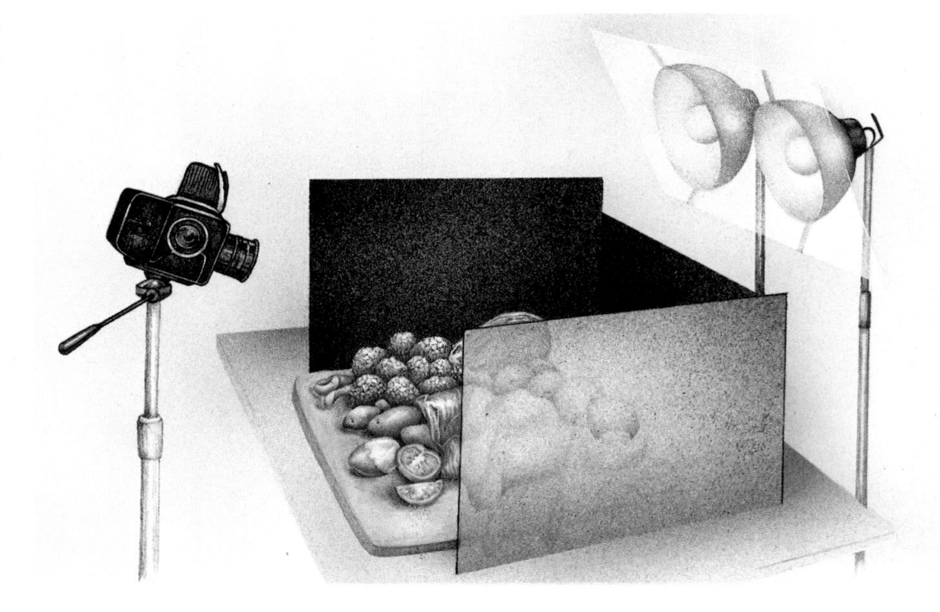

portions of a transparency away from a solid black tone. This overall illumination should be softened by bouncing the light off a white umbrella, or a sheet of white card or polystyrene.

Once you have arranged the main light for the highlight and a second, soft light for the overall exposure, stand back and look at the scene. If the shadow areas look too muddy and dark, you may need to provide gentle rim lighting to provide some separation of the planes in the picture. This can be sidelighting, backlighting or toplighting, set so that the light just catches the perimeter or the subject, but does not illuminate the shadows—if the rim light is overdone, the low key effect is lost.

Exposure readings for low key pictures should be made in the same way as for high key, using the incident light method, or a grey card. Remember, though, to take the reading from the fully lit part of the subject, and not from the shadow areas. Since low key lighting is even dimmer than high key, this is very important—bracket exposures to ensure good results.

If your technique is right, you should be able to process and print low key pictures in the normal way. Shadow detail is important, though, so if you are printing in black and white, concentrate on the shadow areas of the print.

High and low key treatments are, first and foremost, creative techniques. They are not an end in themselves, and they become monotonous if used over and over again. Not all subject matter benefits from either of the two techniques and you need to use some discretion when picking out what to photograph. Nevertheless, with the right subject, either treatment can produce an exciting, unusual picture.

High key head
For this picture, the lighting was much more complex. The main light was the same sheet of diffusing material, but this time placed directly above the camera and lit by two photofloods. Plenty of soft fill-in lighting was provided by bouncing the light from two more floodlights off the white studio walls. The background, a roll of white seamless paper, was lit by floodlights on either side. Finally, a small floodlight on a boom was positioned above the model's head to lighten her hair still further, and this was covered by tracing paper to soften its beam. To prevent a deep shadow forming under the chin, the model held a large sheet of white polystyrene, which acted as a reflector, throwing some of the light up into her face

The moods of daylight

Wherever you live, the weather is rarely the same for very long. Sooner or later, the wind changes direction and blows away the clouds or brings the rain, if only briefly. Just as the quality of light changes through the day, so changes in the weather throw a different light on the landscape. The changing moods, the changing shadows and the changing colours offer tremendous creative scope. But to exploit it properly you must be able to handle the technical problems that each type of weather presents.

Traditionally, brilliant sunny days have been the time to take photographs. With the sun shining over your shoulder, the subject is strongly and brightly illuminated. Strong lighting like this used to be essential for the proper recording of the image, but with the development of increasingly versatile film and equipment, pictures can be taken under virtually any light. In fact, strong sunlight creates its own problems and for high quality results demands special techniques—these are explained fully earlier in this chapter (pages 22 to 25).

Cityscape ***Clear skies with little cloud can produce a variety of lighting conditions. Evening light gives warm hues to buildings***

Clouds

When clouds begin to appear in the sky, but the sun continues to shine brightly, it is difficult to see any difference in the quality of the light. Yet the light that falls on the ground is subtly modified by the presence of clouds and it is sometimes worth taking this into account. Clouds scatter the light passing through the atmosphere. This reduces the total light reaching the ground minimally but sometimes significantly. More importantly, clouds help to diffuse the light, reducing its intensity slightly and throwing it into places that were in shadow before. In pictures where shadow detail is important, this can be valuable. And if you want to shoot portraits in strong sunlight, it may well be worth waiting until the sky is just a little cloudy. If, however, the sun goes behind a cloud, the effects on the quality of light are profound.

When the sun goes in behind a cloud, the overall colour temperature—that is the amount of blue light in the atmosphere—rises dramatically. The colour temperature is about 5500K on a totally cloudless day, but when the sun is temporarily hidden behind a cloud, much of the light comes from the blue sky and the colour temperature can be over 6500K. Unless you compensate for this, colour photographs will have a strong blue cast.

One solution is to wait for the sun to re-emerge, but this is not always possible, nor even desirable. The opportunity for the photograph may also evaporate as you wait. On the other hand, you may want to take advantage of the more diffuse lighting available when the sun is behind the clouds. In either case you will need a correction filter for colour film.

Because your eyes do not compensate fully for the change, full correction with a strong amber filter of the 81 series (81B or 81C) usually looks unnatural. Unfortunately it is difficult to generalize because many factors influence colour temperature as well as the cloud cover. For example, a high proportion of the light is blue even on cloudy days, so the colour temperature in the shadow of a building or beneath a tree could be very high. This sort of situation would probably call for a combination of 81A and the stronger 81B. Normally, though, one is adequate.

When the wind is very strong, the clouds move very quickly and deep shadow can, as the clouds obscure the sun, alternate rapidly with brilliant sunshine. When the light is changing so fast, it is usually best to take an average meter reading from the scene and make a number of exposures.

When the sky has both clear blue areas and clouds, its pictorial impact can be increased by using filters. Polarizing filters will increase the contrast between blue sky and clouds with colour film, while yellow, orange and red filters will have a similar effect on black and white pictures. Graduated filters that fade from grey, or a colour, into clear can also be particularly useful. These darken or tint a cloudy sky dramatically while leaving the landscape unaffected.

Overcast skies

A low level cloud cover produces even, sombre lighting and increases colour temperature slightly. In such conditions you will need an 81 series warming filter to compensate when using colour film, but an 81A should, generally, give adequate correction.

Everywhere colour contrast drops, but the effect is particularly noticeable in cities. Exposure settings that are correct for street scenes will generally result in washed-out, bleached looking skies with no visual interest. Unfortunately, there is no simple way of making up for this deficiency and the best solution is to choose your subjects accordingly. Make cloudy days an apportunity for photographing subjects close up and avoid including any sky. Many of these subjects may positively benefit from the soft lighting and the extra light in shadow areas. By underexposing by half a stop you may be able to retain some of the intensity of the richer colours if you are using colour slide film. With black and white negative film, however, you should overexpose slightly—about half a stop.

Tropical rain ***The diffuse light during heavy downpours illuminates subjects from all sides. Even under an umbrella the woman's face is well lit***

Lake scene ***The moment when the sun breaks through clouds to illuminate even part of the scene often produces spectacular and atmospheric pictures***

Rainy days

Lighting conditions when rain is falling are often similar to those under a heavy overcast. The light is bluer than it looks to the naked eye, and frequently very dim. It is tempting to use a high speed (ISO 400/21°) film so that you can use relatively high shutter speeds and narrow apertures for good depth of field. However, when shooting in colour, you really need a slow film to make the most of the weak colours and the generally low contrast. Using low speed film, of course, means that a tripod is an essential piece of equipment if you want to use a narrow aperature to retain reasonable depth of field.

Rainy days also call for colour correction with colour film. But be careful not to overdo it—too much correction can destroy the mood of a colour picture. Although a properly colour balanced picture theoretically requires an 81C correction filter when the sky is heavily overcast, less complete correction will usually give satisfactory colours and at the same time retain the feel of the overcast conditions.

An exception to the generally dim lighting conditions provided by rain clouds is found when the rain is falling from medium level cumulus clouds. These often produce fleeting showers that quickly come and go. Rain and sunshine may alternate very quickly under such conditions, and the contrast between a sunlit foreground and grey rain clouds can give impressive pictures. But correct exposure is not always easy. There is no hard and fast rule, but probably the best approach is to expose for the sky, and allow foreground highlights to burn out.

Lighting is well worth photographing from a safe distance but a tripod is essential. At night it is possible to capture the image of several flashes of lightning by using a time exposure with the camera set on a tripod. For safety and comfort, work from a sheltered position away from high ground. Point your camera towards the storm and set the shutter speed dial to B. With ISO 100 film you need an exposure of about 20 seconds at *f*/16, using a cable release to avoid shaking the camera. With luck you can record several flashes on film during the period that the shutter is open.

Wind

High winds are often accompanied by generally poor lighting conditions, with low light levels that require slow shutter speeds. Even with a strong, heavy tripod held down by your own body weight, it can be difficult to obtain sharp photographs in really strong winds. Yet the changing light conditions with clouds rapidly scudding across the sky can produce dramatic photographs of landscapes and similar scenes. The best solution is to use a heavy tripod and wait for the strongest gusts to subside.

Slow shutter speeds can help to convey the effects of wind on your subject.

Distant hills *Morning mist lying in hills and valleys is accentuated by a telephoto lens, giving a moody softness to this landscape*

Sunlit trees *A shaft of sunlight shining through clouds (right) gives these trees prominence in the scene. Work fast to capture such moments*

Snowscape *Snow can easily fool a light meter into underexposing the picture. Use an incident or grey-card reading if possible.*

Country road *Dark rain clouds make a striking background to a sunlit road. No filtration is necessary for such a scene*

Blurred leaves and branches can give powerful impression of the wind, but you must make sure that normally immovable objects, like heavy tree trunks, are sharp.

Snow

There is more to snow and ice than traditional Christmas card scenes. Grey snow-bearing clouds, for instance, can produce striking lighting effects. With an overcast sky, freshly fallen snow produces very soft, shadowless lighting and still, tranquil landscapes.

Exposures in snowy conditions are best measured by close-up readings or by incident readings taken with a separate hand-held exposure meter. An overall exposure reading from the entire scene will generally give underexposed results, since the meter will be misled by a large area of white snow.

Under an overcast sky, snow-covered fields seem brighter than the clouds above. This is an illusion, but you can artificially create the effect by fitting a graduated grey filter to your camera to darken the sky. The cloud cover over snowy landscapes is usually very pale and blank-looking, and any devices that can add interest to an otherwise dreary expanse of sky are worth using—graduated colour filters for example.

Contrast in snow covered landscapes can be exceptionally low, because the ground acts as a reflector to fill in shadows from below. Low humidity after snowfall usually means crisp, clear visibility. The scattering of light from many directions by snow and clouds means that subject detail will be clearly visible.

Nevertheless, snow scenes often turn out very blue on colour films, particularly if the subject is not lit by direct sunlight. On bright sunny days, shadows on the snow turn deep blue as they reflect light from the blue sky. There is no way you can correct this by filtration, for any filtration you apply to warm up the shadows will add a colour cast to the brilliant white snow in the sunshine. This is nothing much to worry about, for people expect the shadows on snow to be blue. However, when your main subject is not the snowy landscape, it may be worth trying to correct. If, for instance, you want to take a portrait with your subject standing in shadow, uncorrected flesh tones will be unpleasantly blue. In this case, you need a warming filter to restore the skin to its natural colour. An 81EF is sometimes necessary, but an 81B or C will usually warm up the skin tones sufficiently without destroying the atmosphere of the scene.

Summer landscape *Clouds cast a rapidly changing pattern of shadows on the ground on a sunny but windy day*

Fog, mist and haze

Reducing visibility and weakening both contrast and colours, fog, mist and haze seem at first glance to present enormous problems for the photographer. Yet there are a number of simple techniques to reduce their effect and there is no reason to feel restricted by this kind of weather. Indeed, with their distinctive lighting, fog, mist and haze can provide ideal conditions for certain shots.

Fog, mist and haze all serve to scatter the light from the sun, taking the edge off fine detail and dramatically reducing contrast. While for most photographs this is a disadvantage, the soft, diffuse lighting can often be more attractive than direct sunlight, particularly for close-ups. A conventional outdoor portrait is normally better without hard shadows, and a hazy sun can be an ideal light source. It gives definite, but soft, modelling to the face. Small landscape details, such as flowers, often benefit in the same way.

Because fog, mist and haze have greater effect over a distance, they all, to some extent, enhance the impression of depth in a scene. Backgrounds are weaker, softer and brighter, and these conditions help foreground objects to stand out more clearly. This effect is known as *aerial perspective,* and can give a valuable sense of distance to a landscape. To take full advantage of aerial perspective, compose the image in such a way that distinct elements of the scene are visible at different distances from the camera—foreground detail, trees in the middle distance and distant hills on the horizon. A moderately wide-angle lens usually helps to reinforce this effect. Any subject that recedes from the camera, such as a road, benefits from this treatment.

On a hazy day, aerial perspective is quite gentle, but in mist and fog it

Early morning ***By exposing for the bright sky, the photographer has used the mist to hide unwanted detail, and made an abstract pattern from the trees***

Blue bridge ***In thick fog, your subject may be invisible until it is almost on top of you. The answer is to move in close and use a wide angle lens***

becomes so pronounced that the landscape can appear to be made up of several distinct planes, stacked in front of each other. Apart from the graphic possibilities that this offers, it has two very practical uses in photography: it both isolates and conceals. By separating objects visually from their backgrounds, fog and mist provide clear, uncluttered outlines—individual trees, for example, can be isolated within a copse to provide a strong, simple image.

This is a positive use of fog—focusing attention on one subject—but it is also possible to use fog to hide backgrounds and settings that are either ugly or inappropriate. A line of pylons running across the hills in the distance, or the smoke stacks of a factory, may be an unavoidable part of the picture, particularly if you have only a limited choice of viewpoint. Here, a light mist will conveniently remove the intrusions from the image. In these ways, mist and fog can be thought of as very selective lighting conditions, so that if you are able to choose the time and day for a photograph, they actually give you some measure of control over your subject.

One of the most attractive features of fog and mist is that, being ground-level conditions, they sometimes appear as just a thin covering over the land, so that tall objects such as buildings and trees appear to rise out of a sea of white. On a foggy day, a high viewpoint can be very rewarding, particularly when the fog is clearing and wisps drift across the landscape. Subtle tonal gradations are possible under these conditions, when the thickness of the fog or mist changes across the scene.

Telephoto haze *By using a telephoto lens lens, you can exaggerate the effects of mist and use it to give a strong sense of depth to a picture*

Graininess is also enhanced by fog and mist, simply because they provide broad areas of continuous tone, and you can make a positive feature of this in the photograph. To exaggerate graininess, it is better to use black and white film. A high energy developer, particularly if you use it for push-processing, accentuates the grain even further, as does enlarging a small detail of the negative.

You can also emphasize grain when using colour film, though not as successfully as with black and white. Choose an ISO 1000 film—either negative or transparency—and confine the subject to the central portion of the frame. By enlarging the image more than usual the grain pattern becomes quite prominent.

If you use colour slide film, you can increase grain size in the same way as you can with black and white film—by push processing. It is relatively simple to push process colour slide film at home, but most professional colour laboratories can do it for you, provided you ask for the service when you take the film in to be processed.

There are a number of other ways in which you can enhance the atmospheric effect of fog and mist. A telephoto lens makes the conditions seem more intense, while a wide-angle lens gives a better sense of aerial perspective. Haze, because it scatters blue and ultraviolet light most of all, can be enhanced on black and white film by using a blue filter, such as a Wratten 47. An effects filter, which softens the image to give an impression of mist, is sometimes useful, and a graduated mist filter can be used to affect only the distant part of the view, making it more realistic. To lower the contrast of a foggy picture even more, you could try overexposure and underdevelopment.

Cutting through the mist

Despite the creative opportunities that fog, mist and haze offer, there are also many occasions when they are a nuisance. This is particularly true of haze—being less definite than the other two, it offers less scope for giving an unusual treatment to a picture. However, haze is more useful to a number of photographic techniques, principally because, unlike fog and mist, it scatters light selectively. The suspended particles in haze are so small that they scatter the shorter wavelengths—principally blue and ultraviolet—more than the rest. This is why a distant horizon often appears blue. Unfortunately, films are more sensitive than our eyes to blue and ultraviolet light, so that the effects of haze are more pronounced in a photograph than in the view itself.

Filters can do much to reduce the effect of haze. With black and white film, any filter that reduces blue gives some improvement, orange more than yellow, and red most of all. But the greatest

Rocking chairs *Dense fog conceals ugly background detail, and you can use it to draw attention to the interesting shapes of objects close to the camera*

Mist on the water *Low lying mist soon disperses, so rise early. Choose a camera angle where the mist is lit from the side by the first rays of sun*

Cutting haze with infrared

One dramatically successful way of eliminating haze in a distant view is to use infrared-sensitive film. This film is manufactured with an extra sensitivity to the invisible wavelengths beyond red—those that are least affected by scattering in the atmosphere. Infrared film is, however, also sensitive to other wavelengths, so that to get the best from it, you must use an appropriate filter. Black and white infrared film is sensitive to violet, blue and red, as well as to infrared, while colour Ektachrome infrared is sensitive to green, red and infrared—rather than blue, red and green, as in a normal colour film. Since it is the ultraviolet and blue end of the spectrum that contributes most to the effects of haze, a yellow or orange filter, at the very least, is essential.

Colour infrared film has, in addition to its haze-clearing properties, the more startling effect of false colour, particularly with living vegetation, which it records as red or magenta instead of green. Black and white infrared film, on the other hand, can be used as a more normal substitute for regular film: with a red filter such as a Wratten 25 or 29, some of the visible spectrum contributes to the picture, but with an 87 filter, which is visually opaque, the haze penetration and the contrast are intense. In both cases, vegetation appears very bright, because the green chlorophyll in plants reflects infrared light very strongly. For exposure, follow the instructions packed in the film, bearing in mind that your exposure meter is not sensitive to infrared. An example of haze penetration with IR film is shown on page 42.

Most lenses are designed to focus only visible light, and with infrared film you must focus a little nearer than you would normally. Most lens mounts are marked with a red dot next to the focusing index—use this as your new focusing mark.

While infrared film is ideal for eliminating haze, it actually gives worse results than normal film in fog; the water droplets are so large that they reflect all wavelengths, especially infrared.

Infrared cityscape *Dust particles which scatter light and cause haze have no effect on infrared. But by using a special film and a filter which blocks all wavelengths except IR, haze can be virtually eliminated. The lower picture was taken on conventional film*

effect is given by a Wratten 29 deep red filter. Unfortunately, with such a darkly coloured filter in place exposure must be increased by four stops.

With colour film, really effective haze penetration is not possible because strong coloured filters cannot be used. An ultraviolet filter helps a little, but its effect is only really obvious at high altitudes, where ultraviolet scattering is strongest. Some ultraviolet filters have a pale yellow tinge to counter the blue scattering visible when a telephoto lens is used for a distant view. However, when using a telephoto, the simplest way to control haze is to carefully choose the time of day and the viewpoint. Generally, haze is weakest early in the morning and strongest in the early afternoon. It is also most obvious with backlighting. If you have the choice, select a camera position where the sun is behind or to one side of you.

Depending on the camera position, you may find that the most effective filter is a polarizer. Although better known for its more obvious properties of darkening blue skies and cutting reflections from non-metallic surfaces, one of the most useful functions of polarizing filters is to eliminate reflections from haze particles—at least, those at right angles to the direction of the sun —and to improve contrast and colour saturation. Contrast can also be improved by using an effective lens hood.

With both black and white and colour film, you can heighten contrast further by increasing the development time by about 50 per cent. If you are prepared to accept the extra graininess, the slight increase in contrast may be valuable.

Nevertheless, the most certain way of avoiding the effects of haze is to move close to your subject. The nearer you are, the less atmosphere and so the fewer particles there are in front of the camera. This means, where possible, using a wide angle lens. Also, because subtle and neutral hues make it easy for the eye to distinguish the bluish cast that is characteristic of haze, a brightly coloured subject is better.

Exposure control

Because of the light scattering effect, fog and mist can often present problems with exposure. Fog and mist generally bring an overall bright tone to a scene, so that if you follow your meter's reading unswervingly, you run the risk of an underexposed photograph. Exposure meters average the light that falls on their cells from different parts of the subject, and deliver a setting that produces a mid-toned image. If most of the picture area is taken up with white mist, the exposure that your meter recommends results in an image that is grey rather than white. The solution is to decide how much lighter than average you want a foggy scene to appear, and increase the exposure accordingly. The exact amount depends on the particular situation, but generally an extra one or one and a half stops gives good results. However, if you want to capture the gloom of a misty day, follow the meter reading. If, as an experiment, you take a range of bracketed exposures of a fog-bound view, you should find that several look acceptable—what alters is the mood of the picture.

Because fog and mist tend to produce soft, muted colours, any colour cast is immediately obvious. The colour temperature of light on a foggy day is high—about 7500K—and unless some correction filtration is applied, this results in a pale blue cast. Some films produce a heavier cast than others, and all the Ektachrome emulsions look particularly cool in overcast or misty weather. The solution is to use an 81 series filter—an 81A, 81B or 81C—all of which warm up the picture and eliminate any blue cast.

Finally, it is important to look after your equipment carefully in fog and mist. The air in these conditions is heavily saturated with water, and condensation is often a problem particularly if your camera is cold. Use a soft dry cloth and lens tissues to remove droplets as soon as they form, not only from the surface of the lens, where they will spoil the image, but from the entire body; if not, water may penetrate the mechanisms. Waterpoofing the camera in a plastic bag is usually unnecessary, but it is important to keep your camera in a shoulder bag except when you are actually taking a shot.

Learning to exercise some photographic control over weather conditions such as these, either by accentuating their most useful characteristics or suppressing those that you do not want, extends the range of conditions under which you can successfully take good photographs. This in turn gives you the opportunity to explore landscapes and other outdoor subjects in a variety of ways, rather than just in stereotyped 'good weather'.

Chapter 3
ARTIFICIAL LIGHT
Light sources

Shop interior ***Film colour balance need not always match the light. Daylight film was used here to good effect with the warm predominantly tungsten lighting***

To the human eye, colours tend to look much the same in every light—a red pen is red and a blue pen is blue in both daylight and electric light. But there are significant differences in the colour of every type of light source, and an object that appears one colour in fluorescent light is a slightly different colour by candlelight. While the eye quickly adapts to changing light and may not see these colour variations, they may be only too obvious on film unless you make appropriate adjustments.

An earlier chapter shows how to correct for variations in the colour of daylight (see pages 34 to 37), but it is just as important to correct for the differences between various types of artificial light otherwise your pictures may turn out with an unpleasant colour cast.

Good colour balance is particularly crucial if you are using colour slide film because it is virtually impossible to adjust the colour during processing. But even with negative film, it is worth trying to get the colour correct when you are taking the picture—if the colour is nearly correct, filtration for printing will be that much easier and if the colour is too far out, it may be impossible to correct even with the strongest filters.

Techniques for colour correction of artificial light sources are, like those for daylight, relatively straightforward, consisting largely of matching the film to the light source as closely as possible and making further adjustments with filters placed over the lens. With artificial light photography, however, you have additional scope for correction because you can often adjust the light source. You may be able to change the light source completely, or adjust its colour with the aid of filters placed over the bulb or reflector.

The problems with colour correction of artificial light come in deciding what correction needs to be made. It is essential, therefore, to identify your light source or light sources. Beware of mixed light sources, though. If you are shooting indoors, for instance, daylight may be coming through the window and mixing with the electric light. Mixed lighting should be avoided if possible.

For indoor work, there are four major types of light—tungsten studio lighting, domestic light bulbs, fluorescent light, and flash—though there are many others such as candles or gaslamps. Artificial light outdoors, however, is much more varied and often hard to identify. Street lamps differ and may use, for instance, sodium, mercury vapour, tungsten, gas, or oil. Only once you are sure of the type of light source can you begin to make corrections for the type of cast they give.

Tungsten studio lighting

Like many forms of artificial light, tungsten studio lights—such as photofloods and 'photographic' lamps—produce a light that looks almost as white as daylight but in fact has a much lower colour temperature; that is, it has a much lower proportion of blue light. Pictures taken in tungsten light on daylight balanced slide film, therefore, have a rather orange cast.

The orange cast from tungsten lighting can be attractive, giving a warm cosy look to the scene and adding colour to skin tones, and you may not always want to correct for it. However, in most circumstances the cast is much too strong and must at least be partially corrected.

Perhaps the simplest correction to make is to buy film balanced for certain kinds of studio lighting. Both colour slides and colour negative films can be bought in versions that are balanced for tungsten studio lights. Colour slide films for studio lighting are normally referred to as Tungsten or Type B films; the colour negative films are usually referred to as Type L. Both these films are designed to give the correct colour balance with photographic lamps at 3200K. These films give fairly good balance with most tungsten studio light and you will rarely need to make any other corrections.

If for any reason you wish to use daylight balanced film, you must use filters. You can place filters over the lights, but if all your studio lights are similar it is far easier to use a filter over the lens. Unfiltered, daylight slide film gives a very orange cast, and to correct you must use a deep blue filter, such as the Kodak Wratten 80A.

Unless you have TTL metering, you must remember to make the necessary exposure adjustments whenever you add a filter.

For nearly all your studio shots, either tungsten balanced film or daylight film with an 80A filter give good results, but there are times when you want the colour balance absolutely perfect. On these occasions you may have to make further adjustments.

First, you must discover what colour temperature your lights run at. Photographic lamps are normally rated at 3200K and may need no special treatment, but photofloods are slightly bluer and are rated at 3400K. So, when using photofloods, many photographers would recommend a pale pink 81A filter to remove the blueness with tungsten film, or an 80B filter with daylight film.

Unfortunately, even this extra care does not ensure perfect colour because the lights cannot be relied upon to stay at their rated colour temperature. Manufacturers of photofloods, for instance, only guarantee that their lamps are within 100K of 3400K, but no closer. Even if you could buy a perfectly rated bulb it would have to be run constantly at the correct voltage. Unfortunately, most domestic electricity supplies vary noticeably in voltage from time to time. You can buy special voltage stabilizers, but these tend to be very expensive.

The colour temperature of studio lamps also varies with their age—photographic lamps, in particular, tend to redden as they get older. Again, you can buy special intensifiers that increase the voltage to maintain the colour as the bulb gets older, but these are an unnecessary expense for the amateur. A final point to remember is that colour temperature also varies with how long the light has been on.

There is little you can do to overcome these variations unless you have an expensive colour temperature meter, but you can keep them to a minimum by taking certain precautions. First, avoid plugging any other electrical appliance into the socket that supplies your lights. Second, whenever you buy new photographic lamps, let them burn for 15 to 20 minutes before you take any pictures because when new they are slightly bluer than the rated 3200K. If you can afford to, it is also a good idea to replace bulbs after five sessions. But there is no need to discard the old lamps altogether: they can be used for black and white work with good results.

If you take these basic precautions, and make the adjustments recommended above, there is no reason why you should not achieve good if not perfect colour balance on every shot. Problems only arise when you get reflections from strongly coloured surfaces. Keep your subject well away from such strong colours unless they contribute positively to the image.

Normal domestic lighting, however, may be slightly harder to deal with.

Boardroom *Tungsten balanced film was used in daylight to give a cold blue cast. But a desk lamp directed on the face improved skin tones*

Domestic lighting

The problem with average domestic lighting is that it can take so many different forms. Although it is normally in the form of tungsten bulbs, these can be anything from 15 watts to 200 watts and upwards. Each wattage gives a different colour temperature—a 25W bulb, for instance, gives out a light of about 2600K while a 200W bulb may work at about 3000K. Colour temperature varies between individual bulbs of the same wattage even more than it does with photofloods.

If you are working at home, colour temperature may also be affected by the colours of the furnishings and decoration, and the colour of the lamp shade.

With all these complications, it is clearly impossible to achieve perfect correction. Fortunately it is rarely needed. People are used to wide variations in the colour and appearance of domestic rooms and so will not usually be upset by minor colour casts. In fact, an orange colour cast may actually give an attractive warmth to the picture.

Nevertheless, if you want your pictures to look fairly natural, you must make some sort of correction. Domestic tungsten lighting is very yellow, so when correcting you should aim to reduce the yellow content. Using tungsten film or daylight film with an 80A filter will eliminate most of the yellow and in many instances this will be adequate.

If results are still too yellow, however, you may have to use an 82A filter with the tungsten film. You could use the 82A in combination with 80A and daylight film but two filters restrict the amount of light reaching the film considerably and

Matching film and light source *A test model consisting of a white subject (the bust) and a multi-coloured object (the butterfly) was photographed on daylight and Type B colour slide film, with a variety of different filters and light sources. The results show that there is very little practical difference between the colour of the light from 3400K photoflood bulbs and that from longer lasting 3200K photographic bulbs. But it can be seen that even with the manufacturer's recommended filtration, results on daylight film are inferior to those on tungsten film*

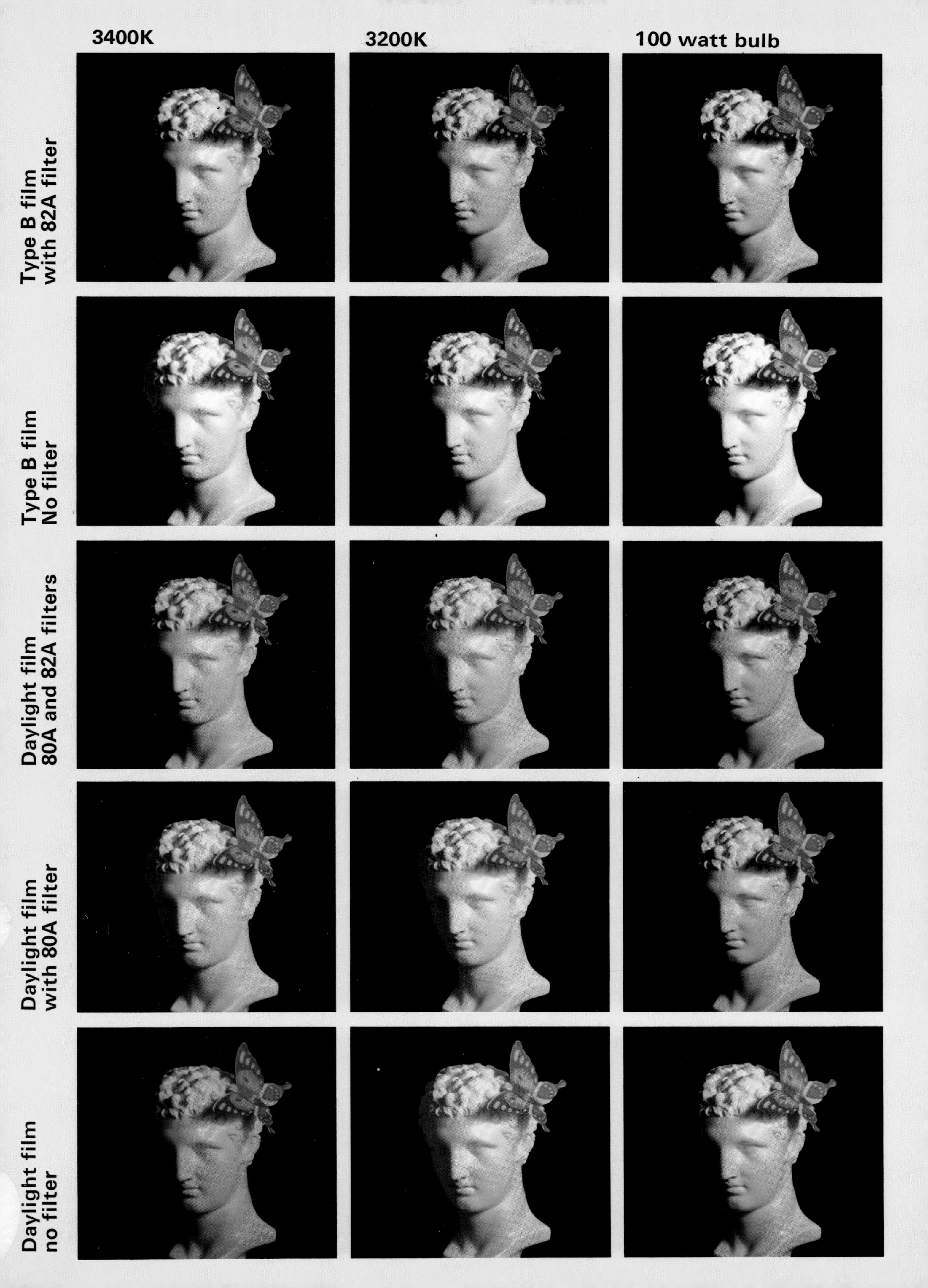
3400K
3200K
100 watt bulb
Type B film
with 82A filter
Type B film
No filter
Daylight film
80A and 82A filters
Daylight film
with 80A filter
Daylight film
no filter

you may need inordinately long exposures to compensate. If you do decide to use to use a combination of filters, it is best to use gelatin filters because they are much thinner and will have less optical effect on the film.

Fluorescent lights

If you often take pictures in any public building, such as a shop or office, you will almost certainly come across fluorescent lighting. Yet fluorescent lighting is one of the hardest of all light sources to correct for. Unlike tungsten light, fluorescent light does not work by heating a thin piece of metal with an electric current, and standard colour temperatures do not apply. So you cannot simply look at the colour temperature and make an appropriate correction.

More importantly, although fluorescent light looks as white as daylight, the basic light emitted by a fluorescent tube is *discontinuous*. Instead of emitting all the colours in varying proportions, it only gives out bands of light of certain wavelengths: some wavelengths are not emitted at all.

If certain colours are missing it may be virtually impossible to put them back, even if you can identify which colours to replace. The fact that pictures taken by fluorescent light have a green cast does not mean that you simply filter out the green, because you might be left with little else. Fortunately, most fluorescent tubes are designed with a continuous spectrum of colours overlaying the discontinuous spectrum. This means that you can make some attempt at correction.

Lighting technicians use a colour temperature meter as a starting point, and correct fluorescent light using colour correction (CC) filters by trial and error, but a simpler alternative if you do not have such a meter is to use a filter specifically designed for correcting daylight colour film in fluorescent lighting. This filter is referred to as FL-D and is available from most filter manufacturers.

Street lamps

Many types of street lamps, like fluorescent light, give a discontinuous spectrum and are therefore very difficult to correct. In fact, there is no correction you can apply to give correct colour rendition in sodium lighting because if you put a filter over the camera lens, you filter out all the illumination in the scene. If you want to take colour pictures in sodium lighting, therefore, all you can do is illuminate the scene with a flash.

There are a number of different types of streetlight in general use, easily recognized by their colour and appearance.

The most common streetlights are mercury (blue–green) and sodium (orange–yellow). Sodium lights are produced in two varieties—low pressure and high pressure.

Mercury streetlights have a spectrum which consists of several bright lines of colours of varying strength, with virtually no red content at all. It is therefore impossible to filter the light to produce a white result, since there can never be enough red. The exact colour which mercury streetlights appear on film depends on the lamps themselves and the type of film used.

While they will always show a blue–green cast, they do give a certain amount of colour rendering to their surroundings.

Low pressure sodium lamps, however, are almost completely one pure colour, yellow–orange. As a result, different colours are indistinguishable in their light. Examine a full spectrum under sodium lighting and you will see it solely in different tones of yellow.

Again, it is impossible to filter the colour of low pressure sodium lamps, and any photograph taken solely by their light will appear the same colour as the lamps.

High pressure sodium lighting has a much mellower pink colour. While it has a strong yellow content, there are enough other colours to give a reasonable colour rendering, and for this reason these lamps are often used in city centres—where it is felt desirable to provide lighting that shows colours.

High pressure sodium light is fairly close to tungsten lighting in its characteristics, so for most purposes either artificial light film or daylight film with an 80B filter will be adequate. For perfect results, 'fine tuning' using colour correction filters is needed. Streetlights of this sort tend to vary widely in colour, so the correction which you establish for one particular lamp may be quite wrong for another lamp of the same type some way down the street. For most purposes, however, it is not important to fine tune the colour in this way as viewers will not expect pink street lighting to give white results.

As a general rule, when making colour corrections it is better to err on the warm side, with a red or magenta cast, than on the cold side, with a blue or green cast.

Stock Exchange *The green cast caused by fluorescent lights can be extremely difficult to filter out. An FL-D filter gives some improvement, but the result is still far from perfect.*

Shooting at night

Taking pictures in the dark seems a contradiction in terms—and indeed it is, for every photograph needs light. But it is very rare to find yourself in total darkness—other than in your darkroom—so there is generally some chance of a picture even in very low light.

It often happens that pictures present themselves at night, but remain unphotographed either because there was no camera to hand or because there was hardly any available light. Even modern emulsions are not as sensitive to light as the eye, so inevitably it is not possible to photograph some scenes, particularly those involving some action, just as you saw them. But it is often possible to take some sort of shot by using the right technique.

The range of low-light photographs that you might want to take includes street scenes at night, candid photography in dark locations, views of floodlit buildings, illuminations, and dimly lit interiors. And there are special effects which make use of the fact that the only light appearing in the picture is what you put there.

Night scene *Using a long exposure, with the camera on a tripod, produces bright streaks from the head and tail lights of all the passing vehicles*

Flash photography outdoors at night is a subject in its own right which is dealt with in Chapter 4.

In general, night photography subjects divide into those where conventional daytime camera techniques with a hand-held camera are adequate, and those where extra help is needed. The first category includes street scenes in brightly lit areas, some illuminations and interiors. Subjects where there is not enough light for conventional photography include such subjects as moonlit landscapes, streets where there is little light, and occasions where you are not prepared for low light photography and have to use whatever means are to hand.

Hand-held camera

Many low light scenes can be photographed normally using a hand-held camera. It is often necessary to do this: you may be trying to take candid photographs in the street, or there may be some action which you have to keep up with. The limitations are the amount of light available, the speed of your film, the maximum aperture of your lens and its focal length.

With slow films, it gets too dark for normal picture taking shortly after sunset, unless you photograph the night sky. Fast films nowadays, however, allow you to continue somewhat longer in to the twilight, using a shutter speed of 1/60 second and the camera's maximum aperture of, say *f*/2. One normally tries to avoid taking pictures at shutter speeds slower than 1/60 second, but as the light gets dimmer this becomes necessary. It is usually possible for most people to hand-hold exposures of 1/30 and even 1/15 second using a standard lens, with care.

Once you have reached 1/15 second, your first option is to change to a wide angle lens, if you have one. Any blur caused by camera shake will be less noticeable with a wide angle lens. But even this will only allow you to use 1/8 second exposure with extreme care.

Your next option is to rate the film at a faster speed, tolerating the loss of picture quality which this involves. This can only be done with certain films—it is impossible with Kodachrome, and while colour negative films will tolerate some underexposure they cannot be processed specially for higher speeds. Ektachrome and other E6 process films can, however, be push processed by one or two stops, as can most black and white films. You can do this yourself by developing for 30 per cent longer than normal. Alternatively, many processing laboratories will push the film speed for an extra charge.

Using film at 1600 ASA(ISO) in a camera fitted with a wide angle lens, with a maximum aperture of *f*/1.7 and a shutter speed of 1/15 second, will allow you to take pictures in quite poor street lighting, or in dimly lit interiors. You are limited, however, to slow moving subjects. Any subject movement will require a shutter speed of at least 1/60 second for sharp results. Depth of field will also be very restricted under these conditions.

One further option available if you need to take low light level pictures is to use a larger camera format. This will not result in extra light on the film, but it will be possible to use fast film without the graininess becoming excessive, since your negatives or transparencies will be bigger compared to the grain size. Roll film or larger format cameras do not usually have lenses as fast as those on 35 mm cameras, however, so there may be no overall gain. And the extra bulk of the camera may make it more difficult to use in those situations where a hand-held camera is needed.

Using a camera support

If you hold the camera steady by using a tripod or some other support such as a wall or table top, many more things become possible. Exposure times can be as long as desired, which means that you can use slower films for better definition. The limitation, however, is that moving objects will record as streaks, or may not even register on the film at all—though this can be used to advantage.

When using a tripod or camera support, it is advisable to operate the shutter using a cable or air bulb release. These usually screw into the shutter release button and allow you to fire the camera off without touching it. As well as making it unnecessary to touch the camera, a cable release tensions itself against the top of the camera body into which it is screwed, rather than pushing down on to the tripod itself. This also helps to prevent vibration.

A cable release at least 30 cm long is desirable. Air bulb releases are generally at least 2 metres long, so the photographer can be some way from the camera operating it.

Most cameras these days, other than the simplest, have facilities for long exposure times. Most often there is a 'B' setting, either on the shutter speed dial, or as an alternative to the automatic exposure setting. With the camera on 'B', the shutter stays open for as long as the shutter release is pressed. If you want to give exposures longer than a few seconds, it is a good idea to use a cable release with a screw lock on the end. The procedure is to press the cable release to open the shutter, screw the

Passing clouds *At night in a moonlit landscape, time exposures can transform a picture. Here the movement of the clouds has spread them across the frame*

Spaghetti junction *A high viewpoint sometimes produces a picture which is totally different to one taken at ground level—these roads look map-like*

Dinner party *With fast film, it is possible to take pictures even in dim lighting. The exposure here was 1/30 sec at full aperture—f/2—using a standard 50 mm lens*

Candlelight *Wide angle lenses can be used without danger of camera shake at even slower shutter speeds. Switching to a 28 mm f/2 lens made this shot possible at 1/15 sec*

locking knob tight, and leave the camera for as long as desired. When the time comes to close the shutter, hold a finger against the cable release end, undo the screw lock and close the shutter by relaxing the spring tension of the cable release. This prevents the violent jerk which may happen if you simply undo the screw lock.

If an unwanted object seems about to enter the field of view during the exposure, you need not end the exposure prematurely. If the surroundings are dark enough you can interrupt the exposure by holding a dark card, cloth or even a hat over the lens. As long as you do not disturb the camera, you can remove it when the object has gone.

Party snaps *When your subjects are moving, flash is not the only answer. Here the 400 ASA film was pushed by one stop to allow a speed of 1/60 at f/2*

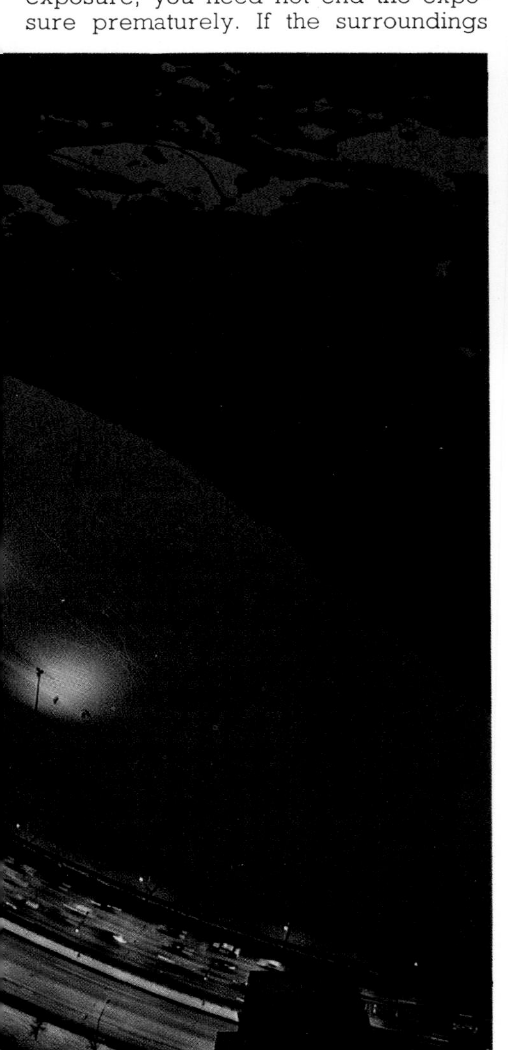

Time exposures of this sort can be used in a wide variety of situations. As well as allowing you to take pictures in places where there is very little light, or where you want to use slow film or a small aperture, they enable you to create special effects. The classic example is the trailed lights of moving cars: it may be necessary to stop down the camera in order to get a sufficient number of trails for an interesting shot. Alternatively you can experiment with a wide range of similar effects by walking along with a torch pointing towards the camera during the exposure.

People in a street will blur in an exposure no longer than 1/4 second, while retaining enough characteristics to show who they are. Dark moving objects may disappear altogether if they have a light background, as the brightness overpowers any trace of them. Time exposures can be used to make a busy street appear completely deserted, or at least populated only by ghostly figures.

By operating a flashgun at some point during the exposure, a sharp but faint image of a person may register within the blur. The exposure which the film receives depends on the aperture it is working at rather than on the total exposure time. If you calculate the flash exposure as you would normally, then you may get overexposed results if the subject in the flash appears against a light background. On the other hand, if it is possible to operate the flash when the subject is against a black part of the picture, the exposure will be normal.

There are, however, additional problems to be borne in mind when using

Dark street *Shop windows at night make an interesting subject, but without additional light the shadows are black and empty, and the glare of the window is all that appears*

Add a flash *Using a flash in addition to a time exposure produces a much better picture. Detail appears outside the window, which still retains a cheery glow*

flash at night. The guide numbers on flash units usually assume that there will be some reflections from walls, so in the open the flash apparently has less power. And anybody with dark hair, complexion or clothes may tend to disappear against a black background. For these reasons, it is not possible to give rules about how to tackle such situations, as the results depend entirely on the conditions at the time.

This technique of using flash can be extended to 'painting with light'. This involves moving around an otherwise dark subject with a portable flashgun, setting it off to illuminate parts of the subject at a time. The operator has to make sure that he or she does not appear silhouetted against the surface being illuminated unless this is specifically required.

Using this technique, you can either use a single flash on each part of the area to be covered, or you can add flashes from the same location to produce more illumination. As for exposure, you can use the guide number system to calculate the aperture needed on the camera for a given flash distance. Then as long as you do not overlap the flashes, you can use the camera as far away from the subject as desired providing the distance from the flash to the subject remains the same as your calculated flash distance. The size of the well illuminated area in the picture, however, decreases as the camera is moved farther from the subject.

This system only works if the flash is pointing more or less away from the camera. Side illumination requires much more exposure, and also runs the risk of allowing the flash to shine directly into the camera.

It is possible to use tungsten lighting, or even a bright torch, to paint a surface with light in the same way, but unless you use the appropriate film or filters (see page 44) the results may have a warm colour when using colour film.

When giving time exposures in this way at night, watch out not only for cars and people entering the field of view, but also for the flashing lights of aircraft in the sky beyond.

In the garden *By leaving the shutter open and 'collecting' a series of images on the film, you can produce a wide range of imaginative pictures*

Exposure and metering

One major problem when photographing at night is that the camera's own meter may not be sensitive enough to give a reading. Alternatively, it may be misled by bright lights in the field of view into giving less exposure than is really needed. In many viewfinders the reading may not even be visible as the numbers can only be seen against the brightness of the subject.

If you are using slow film and want to give a time exposure, many meters will not give an indication as their scales stop at one second. In such cases put the meter on a higher film speed until you do get a reading. Then work out how many stops extra exposure you must give. For example, if your meter does not respond at 64ASA and full aperture, but gives a reading of one second at 500 ASA, then you must give three stops extra exposure (doubling the film speed

Moving subjects *For pictures like this, it is essential that parts of the subject lit by the flash keep still. If they move about, the lights behind can burn out their image*

Freeway in focus *Night scenes are sometimes surprisingly bright, and to allow really long exposures you may find that you have to stop the lens down to a small aperture*

Subway scene *Lighting in many public places is bright enough to permit hand-held candid shots with fast film. Fluorescent lighting gives a characteristic green tint*

gives one stop: the sequence is 125 – 250 – 500). So you must give 8 seconds' exposure on 64ASA film.

To this must be added the complication of reciprocity failure (see page 104). This may result in an 8 second exposure being extended to 30 seconds.

Faced with such problems, many photographers take the easy way out and *bracket* their exposures—that is, they give several different exposures in the hope that one will come out. This is often the best procedure, but it is also good technique to be fairly certain of your starting point.

To prevent the meter being fooled by bright lights, aim to avoid them when metering, and give the indicated exposure even if the lights are to be part of the picture. With fully automatic cameras this may involve guesswork or resetting the film speed dial.

If you cannot read the camera's internal meter, you may have to turn it so as to be able to see the needle or figures against the brightest part of the view. If this is not possible, then guesswork again has to take over.

Working in the dark

As well as there being too little light to take pictures, photography in the dark also means that you may have trouble in operating your camera.

A most useful accessory is a small torch. As well as allowing you to see the camera settings, it can also be used either to throw some light on the subject, or to place on the subject to give you a reference point to focus on. It also comes in handy should you have the misfortune to have to search for some small item of equipment on the ground.

When taking candid shots at night, it is not possible to use a torch for focusing. One solution to this problem is to glue or tape small pieces of matchstick to the focusing ring index mark of your lens. Suitable points might be at the two and four metre marks, for example. Then you can either line up the pieces of matchstick or guess some midway position. With the two focusing extremes, this method gives you four reference points for focusing.

To operate the aperture ring in the dark, get used to how many click stops there are between maximum and minimum apertures. The wider apertures usually have half click stops, so memorize how many there are.

Strips of tape, such as masking tape, can help you distinguish between lenses of similar size in the dark. Stick different numbers of strips round the barrels.

Practice loading and unloading in the dark. To prevent loading a film already exposed, be sure to wind each film fully back into its cassette.

Chapter 4

FLASH TECHNIQUES

Bounce flash

Pictures taken with small flashguns mounted on the camera and aimed straight at the subject are rarely very pleasing. If the light in your pictures always comes from the same direction and has the same character—flat, but with deep, hard edged shadows and pronounced fall-off over distance—then you need a different approach. Taking the flashgun off the camera's flash shoe is the simplest answer, but perhaps the most effective technique is to point the flash unit at some reflecting surface, using the reflected light to illuminate the subject.

This technique, known as *bounce flash* because the light from the flash is bounced off the reflecting surface, can make your photos look much more interesting. It produces a light that is softer and more enveloping, which suits many subjects better than simple, direct flash on the camera.

Using walls and ceilings

Bounce flash from a white surface is as close to natural lighting as you can get with a portable flashgun. Obviously, any white surface reflects light, but a ceiling is usually the most convenient reflector.

The main disadvantage of bounce flash is that you are totally dependent on the location. Ceilings vary widely in height and colour. A ceiling that is dark toned or discoloured by tobacco smoke can absorb a great deal of light. With a high ceiling, the light from the gun has to travel further and may be too weak to properly illuminate the subject.

Many small flashguns are not powerful enough for most bounce work, even though they may be fitted with tilting flash heads. Relying exclusively on bounce flash for lighting interiors other than normal domestic rooms can lead to problems with exposure.

Some automatic flashguns have an exposure confirmation light that blinks if enough light has reached the subject for correct exposure. These can be a useful reassurance. If you have an automatic flashgun, this takes care of the exposure under most circumstances.

If your gun only offers a limited range of aperture settings for use on automatic and none of these is suitable for the distance you are working at or the reflectivity of the ceiling, you may need to switch to manual. Calculate the proper lens aperture yourself, and add the distance the light travels from the flashgun to the ceiling to the distance from the ceiling to the subject. Make an extra allowance for the light absorption of the ceiling. A plain white ceiling normally requires at least an extra stop exposure, but this may vary considerably.

You can make reliable estimates of the necessary correction with experience. Until you have gained this experience, bracket your exposures: make extra shots at one stop more and one stop less than your calculated aperture setting. When working out the correct exposure for manual bounce flash, it is safer to assume that the ceiling is slightly higher and slightly less reflective than it looks.

Bounce flash can create pictorial problems too. If the angle of bounce is too acute, your subject may suffer from heavy vertical shadows. Strong shadows under the eyes and chin can spoil a portrait and are as unsightly as direct flash on camera. Shadows like this are inevitable if you attempt to bounce the

Bounce from a wall *The even sidelight given by bouncing your flash off a wall can often resemble natural daylight from a side window*

Coloured bounce *Beware of coloured walls, especially cool blues and greens. The results will have a cast which may not be what you wanted*

No reflector *Side bounce from a short distance can give deep shadows with insufficient detail*

Silver reflector *A sheet of silver foil held on the shadow side of the subject improves the lighting ratio*

Gold reflector *A more pleasing effect is given to skin tones by using gold-coloured foil rather than silver*

Reflector distance *The amount of shadow fill can be varied by altering the distance from reflector to subject*

flash virtually straight up and down. One answer to the problem is to use a more powerful flashgun and stand further back from your subject, but a better solution may be to bounce the light off a wall rather than a ceiling. In this case, light strikes your subject from the side, giving a similar form of illumination to that from a large window. If you are using colour film, beware of coloured walls. Any light reflected from a coloured wall gives a cast to the subject you are photographing. This is not much of a problem if the wall is pale pink or buff, but green or blue walls can give unpleasant skin tones.

Reflectors

The next logical step after bouncing light off a wall is to use a reflector to direct light into shadow areas. A white sheet pinned or taped to a wall makes a simple and reliable reflector. Sometimes you may want a brighter reflection than a white surface can give. In this case, you need a silvered surface. There are sophisticated reflector sheets, coated silver on one side and white on the other, that fold up small enough to fit into a camera bag. An inexpensive alternative is to stick aluminium foil on to a sheet of expanded polystyrene of the sort sold by builders for home insulation.

Unfortunately, there are few occasions when the subject can easily be placed by a wall, and a wall mounted reflector is not very versatile. At home you can make a mobile reflector by draping a sheet, or a large piece of paper, over a clothes-horse or any suitable piece of furniture. When setting it up, angle it so that light is reflected into the areas that you wish to illuminate. This can be difficult if the flashgun is mounted on the camera, but with an extension cord you can move the flashgun around until you achieve the best illumination.

Outside the home, providing reflectors can be a problem. There are

Bounce boards *These attachments can provide soft frontal light at close distances, and are easily portable*

Soft lighting *The effect given by bounce board flash attachments is particularly suitable for close portraits*

rarely any suitable walls, and it can be awkward carrying your own reflector everywhere. Even if you do persevere and carry a reflector to the location, it can be difficult setting it up. The best solution is to ask a friend to hold your reflector, but if this is not practical you can often get by with sticky tape and spring clips. Bear in mind that reflectors have to be large and conspicuous if they are to be effective. They need to be used quite close to the subject, so it is not really possible to take unposed candid photographs with reflectors.

Bounce boards

Some manufacturers have sought to overcome some of the problems of using bounce flash by making brackets that clip on to their flashguns. These brackets hold a piece of white board that is angled towards the subject to provide a directional form of bounce lighting.

When used properly, these devices can be very effective. The distance from the flash to the bounce surface is constant, and so is the reflectivity of the board. This simplifies exposure calculations considerably if you decide to set your flash manually.

Problems arise when you try to use these reflectors at too great a distance from your subject. Light from the flashgun illuminates the reflector board so that the subject is in effect lit by the large board rather than by a small flash tube.

If you stand close to your subject so that the width of the board relative to the distance from the subject is large, then the light will fall on the subject evenly from many different angles. The effect will be to give a soft frontal lighting if the flash and reflector board are mounted on the camera. But if you move too far back, so that the ratio of board size to distance is smaller, then the effect will gradually become almost indistinguishable from ordinary direct flash.

Bounce boards also tend to be bulky and may not mount very securely on your camera. These drawbacks reduce the usefulness of bounce board attachments for photography outside the home or other more controlled situations. They are most useful for highly mobile subjects such as young children and pets, when you wish to avoid the contrast and hard shadows of direct flash. Their effect is also particularly useful for head-and-shoulder portraits.

Portable bounce *Fitting a flashgun with bounce board attachment to your camera can make your equipment top-heavy, but the results should more than compensate*

Twin tube flashguns
Another attempt by flashgun manufacturers to solve the problems created by direct flash on camera is the twin tube design. Bounce flash from a ceiling usually requires a powerful flashgun so that you can stand sufficiently far from your subject to reduce unpleasantly hard vertical shadows. Twin tube flashguns use a small second flash tube pointing directly at the subject to fill in these shadows and allow you to work close to your subject while still keeping some of the advantages of bounce light. Since you do not need to be so far away, the flashgun itself can be smaller, cheaper, and easier to carry.

A certain amount of thought is needed to use these units effectively. Because they produce results under a wide variety of conditions, it is easy to forget that the main light is supposed to be provided by the bounce tube pointed at the ceiling. If the ceiling is too dark or too far away, the subject will be lit entirely by the direct light of the secondary flash tube and you will be back where you started—using direct flash on camera. In such cases, it is best to accept the inevitable and point the main flash tube at the subject to use the full power of the gun.

Twin tube flashguns provide more attractive lighting than ordinary direct flash units, but the effect they give can become just as routine as direct flash if used too often. Try to vary the way you use these units as much as you can. Remember also that the proportion of bounce to direct flash on which the manufacturer has preset the unit may not suit your pictures. If this is the case, you can make adjustments by taping pieces of opaque card or paper over the flash tubes until the effect is just right to suit your style.

Twin tube flash *A compact compromise between direct and bounce flash, above. The results, below, show agreeably soft, indirect light combined with the greater liveliness of direct flash on the camera. The direct flash helps to fill in the shadows*

Natural flash

Flash is undoubtedly a valuable weapon in the photographer's armoury and in many circumstances it is the only way of achieving a picture. But many photographers will not use it because they feel it destroys the atmosphere of the available light, particularly natural daylight. However, used in the right way, flash can not only be used without upsetting the quality of the available light, it can positively enhance it by controlling contrast, adding detail and improving colour and sharpness.

If you wish to retain the feeling of natural light but wish to use flash to fill in shadows in indoor shots, it is important that the use of flash should not be obvious in the picture. there are a number of ways of achieving this, but it is undoubtedly simplest to keep the flash light weaker than the available light.

Sharp crosses ***Adding flash to the picture not only lightens the shadows, so giving a more reasonable contrast range, but also helps to make the image look sharper. This is because the flash 'freezes' any movement***

Weak flash

With an automatic flashgun the flash can be weakened quite simply by altering the settings. First set the aperture on the camera to give the correct exposure for the light available. Then set an aperture one stop larger on the flashgun dial. If the exposure for the available light is 1/30 second at *f*/4, then you could set the flashgun at *f*/2.8. This means that the flash will be too short to give a full exposure but is sufficient to lighten shadows.

Use a warm coloured filter such as an 81A to reduce the blue highlights produced by direct flash, and try to avoid the tell-tale shadows running back from the subject, either by having no close background, or else one which is so close that the shadows are too small to be noticed. You can either come in very close, so that the light source is effectively larger, or keep back a little, so that all the clues are smaller and so less noticeable.

When you wish to achieve a really subtle effect, you can increase the

aperture setting on the flashgun by two or even three stops. Used like this, the flash will be almost imperceptible but it helps to introduce a little colour, shape and texture into shadow areas and lift the picture generally.

Subtle fill-in flash may also help to make your pictures look sharp because the flash is so brief. The flash exposure does not, therefore, suffer from even a trace of camera shake and this ultra sharp flash image helps to give the whole picture an extra crisp look, especially in hand-held shots.

Another application of weak fill-in flash is to reduce colour balance problems when using daylight film in fluorescent or tungsten lighting. Aim the flash at the important features of the subject so that even if the rest of the picture suffers from a slight colour cast, it may not be noticeable because the focal point is rendered in the true colours. With the flashgun set one stop larger than the camera, the use of flash may be undetectable.

If, for any photographs you wish the flash and available light to be equally balanced, beware of simply setting the flash for the same aperture setting as the available light exposure. This merely results in an overexposed picture. Where the flash duration is brief, it has little effect on the overall exposure. But once the flash exposure is one to one with the available light, it increases the amount of light in the picture considerably. The solution to this problem is simply to reduce the aperture on the camera by one stop.

Using the flash on a one to one basis will of course change the overall effect of the lighting quite considerably, but the existing light may well hold its own remarkably well. One reason for this is that backlighting is more obtrusive than front lighting, but the light from the flash, even when bounced, is usually more frontal than the existing light. Indeed it is the lack of backlighting that often makes flash (on its own) such a limited form of lighting. If you mix flash with available light you can often make use of a window, a table lamp or any other bright source to provide some backlighting. Backlighting not only separates each part of the subject from the background, but puts highlights on to every flat surface, bringing out shape and texture and subtly increasing the tonal range.

Quality control

While the simplest way of keeping pictures taken with flash natural is to use a weak flash you can also control its *quality* so that it looks like available light. To do this, you have to imagine the natural lighting for your subject, and then use the flash to reproduce it. You need to estimate not only the size and power of the light source correctly, but also its distance and angle.

The size is important because the type of shadows, the size of the highlights and the graduation of tone between the two are controlled by the size of the light-source. If you want to make light which, for instance, looks as if it comes from a window, then you need a light source the size of a window. This can usually be done quite simply by bouncing flash from a white wall. The patch of flash on the wall will tend to be the same size as a window. If there is no white wall in the right place, you can bounce the flash off a reflector. This can be either a proper studio reflector, a large white umbrella, or even a white bedsheet, a sheet of white paper or polystyrene, or just a couple of pages of newspaper taped together.

Remember that for bounced flash the autocell on the flashgun has to be pointing at the subject. With some flashguns this is awkward, especially when they are mounted on the camera. An ex-

Backlighting *In the shot above, the flash has played an important part in showing detail in the room. But the available light is still crucial—the light from the fire picks up detail in the face, and the light from the doorway helps to outline the figure and pick up texture in the floor. For the pictures below, it was important to keep the detail in the background, by careful choice of exposure time, to provide a setting for the children, who were in shadow (right) and so were lit almost entirely by flash in the final shot. There is very little mixing of flash and available light as each lights a different area of the subject*

Flash proportions *It is very easy for the flash to dominate the picture, as can be seen from the pictures above. In the top shot most of the light is from the flash, although the daylight from the window (shown in the lower shot without flash) helps to illuminate the face and overalls. In the three shots below progressively greater amounts of flash were used, in ratios of 1:4, 1:2 and 1:1 to the available light. It can be seen how the flash has gradually become more noticeable until it finally destroys the natural quality of the light. The frontal lighting of the flash is artificial and so looks wrong when allowed to dominate*

cellent solution is to have the autocell mounted on the hot-shoe and the rest of the flashgun on the end of a lead, so that it can be held as you wish. Some flash units have autocells which can be unplugged and used in this way, others offer the autocells, or 'remote sensors' as they are also called, separately.

In the same way, when you bounce flash from the ceiling you are, in effect, mimicking strip lighting because the overall effect of many fluorescent tubes is to turn the whole ceiling into one large light source—bounce-flash from the ceiling does exactly the same.

If you use direct flash it looks artificial unless you can position it to imitate some naturally occurring light source. If you want to imitate direct sunlight with a flashgun, take it off the camera and position it above and to the side of the subject, pointing down at the same angle as the sun might be expected to—say around 30°.

Because the sun is very distant, the flash must also be as far away as possible. You can even use a mirror to extend the effective distance if necessary. Obviously this means using a fairly powerful flashgun or else a fast film and a wide aperture, though if the subject is static and you can darken the room, you can fire the flash several times.

If the subject is small it is easier to fool the eye that the light source is infinitely far away. Distant light sources cast virtually parallel shadows. Shadows from nearby lights tend to narrow rapidly. So a nearby source is immediately obvious from the shape of the shadows—particularly with large subjects. As a rule of thumb, if the light source is further than about ten times the width of the area being photographed, the light looks reasonably natural. A light orange filter helps add to the impression especially if the 'sun' is at a low angle. Try a blue reflector in the shadows for a hint of blue sky, but be careful not to overdo it!

Another common light source you can imitate is a table or reading light. In this case the position must be *close,* just as the lamp would be. You may need to place a neutral density filter over the flash head when you are using the auto function, if the flash is less than about a metre from the subject. You can use the flash direct in imitation of a naked bulb, or bounce/diffuse it to look like a shaded lamp. For this purpose a small umbrella is ideal. If you have a remote sensor the flash head can be attached to the handle of the umbrella so that it points into it, and you can position the whole thing close to your subject, right up to the edge of the picture, so that it imitates the quality of a table or standard lamp. With some white umbrellas you can either shine the flash through the fabric of the umbrella which then acts as a diffuser, or else use it to bounce the flash as a reflector. The remote sensor overcomes the problems of working out how much light is transmitted or reflected. Alternatively, you can use a flashmeter.

You can also bounce flash off the television screen to look like the light from a television or bounce it off a sheet of yellow paper placed low down to look like the light from a fire—the possibilities are endless.

As long as you can think of a particular light source which could be in the position you need, you just have to set the flash to that angle, distance and size of source (by bouncing or diffusing) and it will look perfectly natural.

In many situations, there may not be an obvious surface for bouncing the flash from. But it is surprising how many things can be used as reflectors. Virtually any nearby surface can be used. Though strongly coloured objects may give unpleasant casts in colour shots, almost anything can be used in black and white.

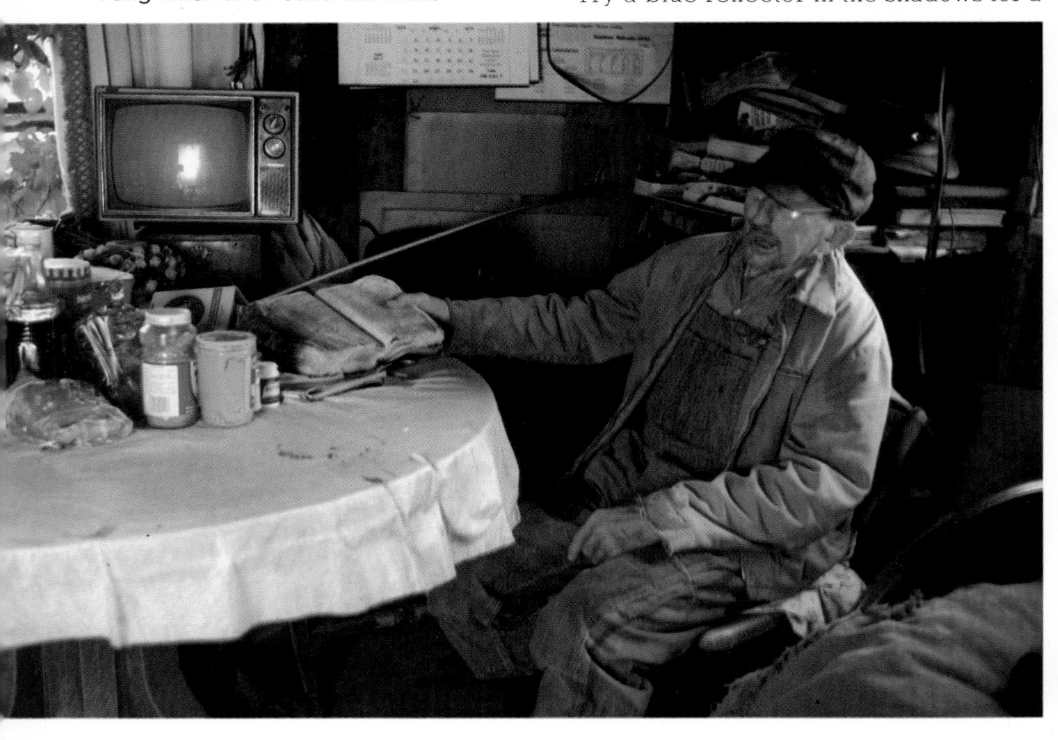

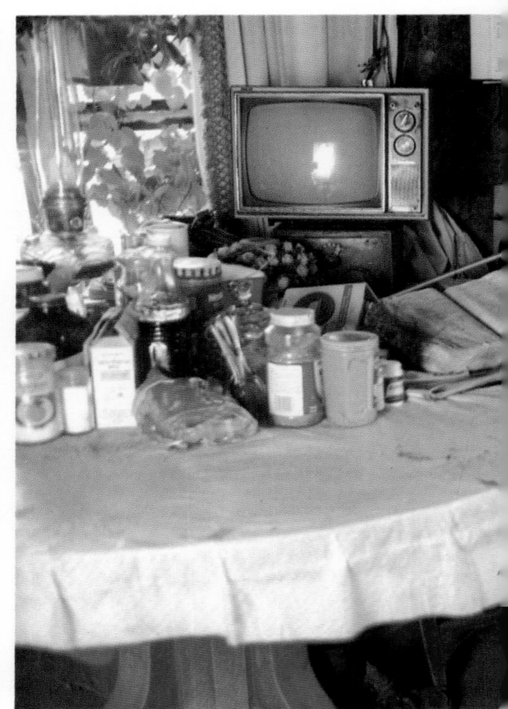

Colour change *Even quite small amounts of flash can be used to clean up colour. Here a small unit was used (right) to remove the unattractive green cast caused by fluorescent lights (left) without changing the atmosphere of the light*

Daylight and flash

When you wish to mix daylight with flash, perhaps to light a portrait against a window, there are different methods of doing it. To obtain a natural result, you could either bounce the flash to one side, to look like the light coming from another window, or bounce from the floor, perhaps from a white sheet if the floor is dark-toned: or from a large reflector behind the camera, to provide the large-source front lighting which might come from a white room. Since the flash is to provide the main light on the subject's face, it is easier to set this first. This is done in the normal way, setting the camera to the same *f*/stop as the flashgun's calculator dial—unless of course, you want it a little darker or lighter than normal.

The daylight is 'controlled' by the shutter speed, and you can make it weaker or stronger just by turning the shutter speed dial. As a starting point take a reading on the general scene outside. This will probably indicate quite a fast shutter speed. If you were to shoot at this setting the light would appear to be the same inside and out and this gives a dull look to the shot.

To brighten the picture, slow down the shutter speed by one or two settings. This will not affect the flash in any way; only the daylight changes. At some point, depending on the exact configuration of the window, and your composition, you will notice that the needle indicates 'correct exposure'. At this point it might be a good idea to check that the subject's face, not lit by the daylight, is still registering 'underexposed' on the camera's meter. Move in close and check: *some* light from the window is sure to reach it. As long as it is still reading 'underexposed', you can go on increasing the shutter speed for a few more stops.

There is no 'correct' setting for the shutter speed in this situation, it just depends what sort of picture you want. In any case the tolerance is enormous. A stop of two either way is not going to do much damage. You may find that the shutter speed is too short to synchronize with the flash in which case you could either select a smaller aperture and work from that, or accept a brighter scene outdoors by lengthening the shutter speed. If the shutter speed is too *long*, either use a tripod, accept a darker outdoor exposure, or, if the flash provides for it, set a wider aperture.

Flash by night

Carnival flash *Here the background, hats and bright clothes have helped to outline the subjects*

Now that flash has become accepted as a tool to give better lighting under many daylight conditions it is easy to forget the more basic use of flash: to take pictures in the dark. And even those who have mastered the technique of using flash indoors and fill-in have trouble taking pictures outdoors at night.

The main problem with using flash outdoors at night is that the resulting pictures never look quite like what you saw through the viewfinder. This is because the quality of flash lighting is quite different from what you normally see. Night scenes are often illuminated by a number of weak light sources: streetlamps, light from doorways or windows or car headlamps. Once your eyes have become accustomed to the dark you can see these. But the light from a flash is much brighter and, usually, harsher. Your camera sees only that and not the weaker available light.

Direct flash

The available light that you can see gives toplighting, sidelighting and backlighting, but the flash on your camera only gives frontlighting. This is the sort of lighting you get when your car headlights pick up a figure in the dark. It shows up colours, patterns or writing very clearly—so it is good for photographing flat, non-glossy objects. But it is bad at revealing overall shape, form and texture, unless the subject is flat, shiny and at right angles to you.

Using frontlighting alone it is easy to lose the edges of subjects. People with dark hair, dark skin or dark clothes may merge into the surrounding darkness. These problems arise both outdoors and in very large interiors with low ambient lighting.

The simplest way to overcome this is to put your subject against a nearby light background, so that any dark areas are outlined against a paler area rather than blackness. If you are out in a field even a bush or hedge will do, as long as your subject is fairly close to it. If there are no hedges about, try getting up high above your subject so that the field itself provides a background. One drawback with this approach is the characteristic hard shadows on the ground that flash often produces. Alternatively, make sure that your subject has white or pale-coloured extremities—a white hat and gloves, for example, would prevent a person's features from merging into the darkness.

Even an automatic flash, which normally adjusts the flash output to give the correct exposure, can often give poor results. One common failing is to forget that every auto flash has a maximum working distance, which is easily exceeded out of doors. But even within its working limits, the auto sensor can still give the wrong results. For example, if the sensor reads only a person wearing light coloured clothes, the result may be underexposure. But if the sensor's angle of acceptance includes an area of dark background, it may try to give too much exposure in an attempt to lighten the scene. So the subject tends to be washed out, particularly if not central in the frame.

Night shots tend to look underexposed, even when they are not, because of the dark background and the lack of fill-in tones. So the only way to be certain of your results is to carry out a trial outdoors at night, using an average subject. Then you can compensate for under- or overexposure in future when choosing the aperture which the flash recommends.

Faced with the problems of uncertain subject brightness and limited flash range, it is tempting to ignore the auto

Disappearing trick *Although exposure here is correct, the dark clothes and hair have merged into the background*

sensor altogether and use the unit manually. This can also lead to problems, but usually the results are more consistent, though underexposed. The guide number and table of recommended apertures are worked out on the basis that the flash will be used in average conditions, with walls and a ceiling to reflect some light. Outdoors, however, up to a stop extra exposure may be needed. Again it is best to experiment with your unit, so that when you need to use it outdoors you can give the correct exposure.

A common outdoor problem is that foreground objects may be very over-exposed. One solution to this is to use a neutral graduated filter over the lens to cut down the foreground brightness, either with the darker half at the bottom or to one side, depending on the picture.

Plane sky *Shooting at dawn or dusk gives you a sky which is just bright enough to outline the subject*

Using available light

Streetlights, bright windows and doors may not give enough light to take pictures by, but often they give enough to pick up the all-important edges of the subject. You could, for example, silhouette your subject against an open door and fill in the detail with flash. With fast film there may well be enough light to do this at the normal flash shutter speed and full aperture, but often you will have to give a rather longer exposure, either because the available light is too dim or because your flash requires a smaller aperture. In this case a tripod is needed, though in some cases a hand held exposure may work—the edges of the flash light area will simply be a little blurred. And if your subject moves during the long exposure, the result will be a dark streak with the sharp flash image within it.

Such a technique can also be used to good effect during twilight. Even if the sky is not bright enough to be properly exposed, it can still give sufficient illumination to outline your subject.

Flash off the camera

If you only have one flashgun you can avoid some of the problems of front-lighting by taking the flash off the camera. You can get some dramatic lighting effects by putting the flash right around to one side, so the subject seems to be illuminated by a floodlight. You could even move the flash behind the subject to give rim lighting—though this will give no front detail.

With the flash on auto you will not need to adjust the exposure. Though the overall illumination of the subject may be less, the parts that are lit will be exposed properly. The shadows will come out black. And with the rimlight it does not matter much what aperture you use—the only effect will be a brighter or a dimmer halo.

If you are using the manual settings on your flash, you only have to concern yourself with the distance between the flash and the subject. Once the subject is correctly exposed it does not matter how far away you shoot it from. This only affects the area exposed on the film—if you are very far away the illuminated area will be rather small in the frame but will be correctly exposed.

Against the wall *Although the background is underexposed, it still helps to give shape to the subject*

Bright face *Giving one stop more exposure brings out the clothes and hair but overexposes the skin tones*

Manual mode *Using the guide number method results in underexposure due to the absence of reflecting surfaces*

Flash bike *Having the flashguns separate to the camera enables the photographer to move around without changing exposure*

Inside light *You can use available light to give a background and still use the flash on automatic*

Tree light *This shot used two flash units—one at the portrait position and one behind the tree to give sidelighting*

Multi-flash

Some of the most interesting effects using flash at night are produced by several flash units working together. The units may be linked using sync leads and multi-way adapters, which can mean long lengths of cable. Alternatively, you can equip each subsidiary unit with a slave cell trigger unit. The main flash unit is triggered by the camera shutter in the normal way, and the other units then fire simultaneously. The flash units need not be very powerful—small units can be bought very cheaply, and are ideal for such use.

The triggering flash can be your main unit, either on or off the camera. It can even be the built-in flash of a pocket or instant picture camera. You may wish to soften and reduce the light output from this by taping a paper handkerchief over it, so that the resulting picture will not appear strongly front lit.

The best location for your main flash is probably the classic portrait position, above and to one side of the camera, though this depends very much on the nature of the subject. With just one secondary flash you can add light to one side, which will give a bright sheen to that side, or you can put the light above and behind the subject. This will tend to create a misty blue beam in the air, while any light behind the subject will give rim lighting. Alternatively, you can illuminate the background to the subject, to avoid the subject's edges merging into the darkness.

For side and rim lighting, you need not worry unduly about the subsidiary flash's output as far as exposure is concerned. Rim and side lighting is expected to appear overexposed, so a stop or two either way has little effect on the final result. But if any two flashes overlap, some calculation or even guesswork will be needed. Remember that if two flashes with the same setting are combined you should reduce the exposure by one stop.

If you have four flashguns you can fix them up at the four corners of the area you want to work in, using tape or elastic bands to attach them to trees, lamp posts or, if you are in a building, to the walls. Point them all towards the centre, but point the slave units at the triggering flash so that when it goes off, they all do. Some slave units are not very sensitive and need to receive a lot of light from the

main unit.

Now you can move around freely taking pictures in any direction, with every one well lit. You are guaranteed backlighting to separate every shape from its background, pick up texture and highlight smoke or steamy breath. As long as you do not shoot with your back too close to any of the units they will not over-light the subject—the autocell on the main flash should automatically compensate for light from the secondary units.

If any of the flash units are in the picture, the results may still be attractive. They will give some flare some burnt-out areas, just as you would get from street lights or other 'natural' night illumination.

Painting with light

Another way to get the flash off the camera is to put the camera on a tripod, lock the shutter open on the 'B' setting and go for a walk round the subject, which must be stationary, firing the flash again and again at different parts. This 'paints' in the picture area by area and is much easier to do than it sounds.

As long as you only fire the flash once at any given point on the subject you can use exactly the same setting as for normal flash. The autocell will adjust the output to give each part the same illumination, or you can fire the gun at the same distance from the subject each time. You can backlight, frontlight and sidelight the same object with a single flash unit in this way. Or you can fill in a whole nearby landscape piece by piece. It does not even matter if you stand in the frame, as long as you are not silhouetted by the flash and you do not get your feet in the way. If no light falls on you, you will not appear in the picture.

If the flash is pointing towards the camera and is in the frame there will be flare, which you may or may not want. And if a figure moves every time the flash is fired their image can be laced through the landscape. All you are doing is building up a single picture from a number of different exposures.

Alternatively, you can fire the flash twice at each part and stop down the lens one stop to give a greater depth of field. If you fire the flash four times you can stop down two stops, eight times and stop down three stops.

Standing closer to the subject with the flash will give a smaller pool of light of course. But if you want to light something big, evenly, like a building, you may have to stand well back and fire repeatedly. If you are back beyond the auto range of your flash you will have to calculate the exposure as before.

As using a long exposure is inevitable, you can add tracer effects from the tail lights of cars, torches, fairground lights, or even fireworks to trace out shapes with light.

Just rim lit *The flash used to give rim lighting can be read by the sensor on the main gun, giving underexposure*

Flash painting *This shot was lit by 15 separate flashes, while the shutter was kept open for three minutes*

High-speed flash

Bullets frozen in flight, balloons bursting, a boot kicking a football—these subjects make fascinating pictures simply because they show clearly things which occur too quickly for us to see. High-speed photography has made it possible to capture these moments but, until recently it was out of reach of the photographic amateur, because of the expense of the highly sophisticated equipment that was needed. But the introduction of automatic 'computer' flashguns has provided a handy source of the very brief, intense flash of light that is needed to stop super-fast action.

Placed close to the subject, these units produce a very short flash almost as a by-product of their exposure control system. This provides the basis for your own work in high-speed photography.

How they work

The idea of using a flash to freeze motion is not new—William Fox-Talbot photographed a whirling newspaper using this method as long ago as 1851. Modern electronic flash units have just made it a great deal easier.

Prairie splash *High speed photography can produce dramatic pictures from the most mundane subjects, such as this shot of a prairie oyster in the making*

In a flap *A computer gun, used with a fairly wide aperture, gives a fast recycling time allowing you to take several shots of a moving object*

Output control *Some flashguns have controls which reduce the flash output, either built in or, as in this case, as an accessory. Lower output gives a shorter flash duration*

plywood board
foam rubber
microswitch
baseboard
sync leads to flash

Breaking eggs *The switch which fires the flash is located in a layer of foam between two boards. The egg hitting the bowl depresses the top board which then presses the switch*

The flash duration of manual flashguns is fixed, and exposure is determined using the familiar Guide Number system, but with automatic models, exposure is controlled by changing the flash duration, and it is this feature that makes these units particularly suitable for arresting motion. With manual guns, the flash always lasts as long as the flashgun's capacitor takes to discharge. This may be as little as 1/100 or even a 1/125 second, but this is not short enough for high speed photography. With an automatic gun, however, the flash can be cut off well before the capacitor is discharged and the flash duration can be reduced dramatically. In an automatic flash, a built-in 'computer' measures the amount of light reflected back from the subject. When this amount reaches a quantity which will give sufficient exposure for a particular film, then the light from the flash tube is cut off. At normal flash-to-subject distances, this cut off point is reached after about 1/1000 or 1/2000 second, but when the flash and subject are very close together, and a fast film and wide aperture are used, the flash is quenched much more quickly. It may only light the subject for 1/20,000 or 1/30,000 second. It is this short duration flash which makes possible dramatic action stopping pictures when the level of ambient lighting is low.

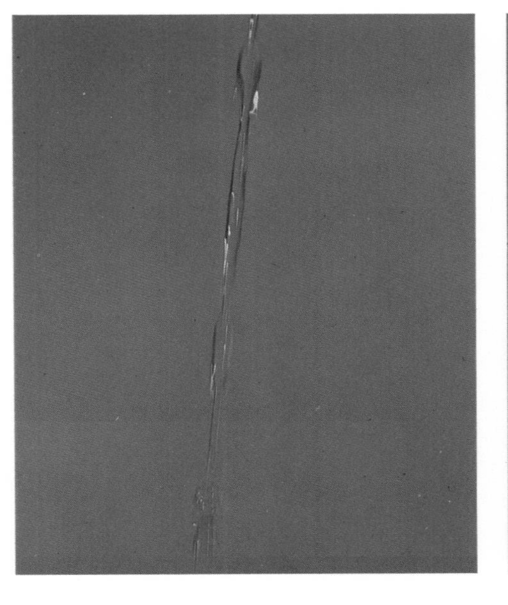

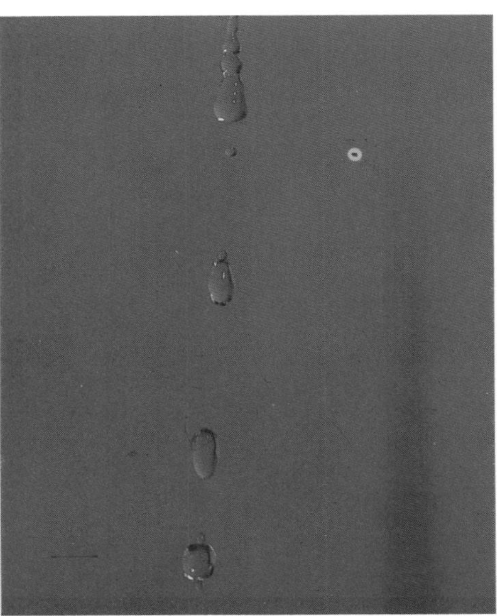

Frozen water *Both pictures were taken with the same flashgun used on its manual setting (left), the flash duration being 1/1000 sec and on its extreme auto setting (right) giving 1/30,000 sec*

Some units have additional features such as half- or quarter-power settings, to allow for greater image control through aperture variation, or to cope with a greater range of flash-to-subject distances. Lower power is used with subjects close to the camera and the use of such a setting will probably give shorter flashes—1/25,000 sec is possible.

For successful high-speed work, the flash must not only be brief and intense, it must also take place at the appropriate moment in relation to the action being photographed. So a triggering device is needed to fire the flash at the right instant. As the camera shutter must be wide open when the event takes place, conventional synchronization is usually unsuitable and it is common practice to take this type of photograph by *open flash methods* where the firing of the flash does not involve the camera's shutter at all.

For open flash photography, the camera shutter is kept open for the duration of the action, using a locked cable release and the B setting on the shutter speed dial. The flash is then fired with an independent triggering device to briefly illuminate the subject at the right point in the action. Providing the room is sufficiently dark (with the

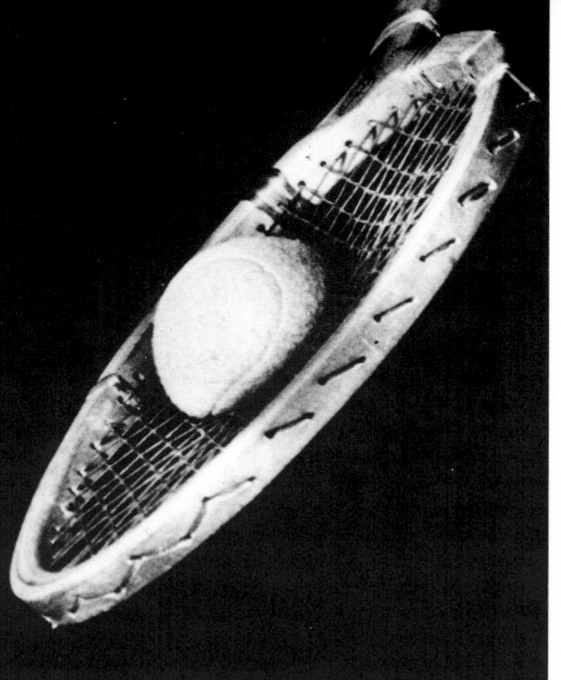

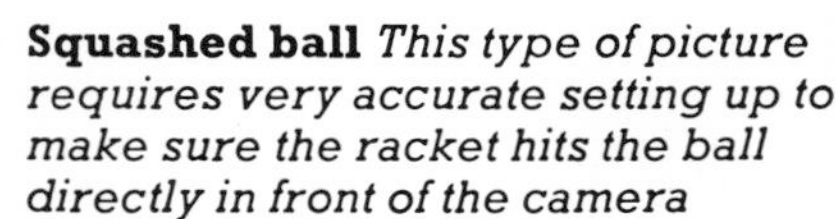

Squashed ball *This type of picture requires very accurate setting up to make sure the racket hits the ball directly in front of the camera*

curtains drawn and the lights off) only the moment when the flash is fired should register on the film. The trigger can simply be a microswitch arranged so that the subject sets off the flash itself at the right moment. This is usually fairly easy to improvise, and an example is given below.

When using this technique, it is important to ensure that the flash fires only once while the shutter is open. With simple automatic flashguns there is no problem: any power not required for film exposure is simply 'dumped' in a black painted flash tube within the body of the gun. The excess energy is therefore dissipated as heat. When one of these flashes is used at a short distance, all of the power stored in the capacitor is used up each time the flash is fired, and the recycling time is always the same—about five to ten seconds—regardless of the flash-to-subject distance.

With energy-saving or thyristor flashguns, however, unused energy is retained in the main capacitor, where it is stored for the next flash instead of running to waste. The recycling time is therefore shorter, and when the subject is very close to the flashgun, it may be almost instantaneous.

In practice

A fairly simple subject to photograph with open flash techniques is a raw egg, in its shell, being dropped into a bowl. The aim is to photograph the egg as it smashes on the bowl bottom.

The flash head is placed at only a short distance from the subject—as close as 60 cm—and both the subject itself and the background (the inside of the bowl) are light in colour. Furthermore, quite a wide aperture is used so that little light is needed to light the shot—though this sometimes creates depth of field problems.

The flash unit and the camera must be set up so that they look down into the bowl and, for reasonable modelling of the egg when broken, the flash-head should be placed at about 90° to the camera axis.

For a subject like this, you might be able to achieve acceptable results with synchronized flash, relying on your ability and quick reactions to release the shutter at the precise moment of impact. But you are more likely to get good results with a minimum wastage of eggs, film and time, if you set up a trigger mechanism under the bowl. The force of the egg hitting the bottom of the container can be used to set off the flash. You can easily build a suitable device from bits of scrap wood, a few light springs or foam plastic, and a microswitch which, when pressed, makes an electrical contact. Connect this switch to the flash unit through a suitable lead (such as a modified flash extension lead) and mount it button uppermost, on a piece of board. Another board is supported over the top of the switch, using springs or foam. The slightest pressure on the upper board, with the bowl on top of it, operates the microswitch and fires the flash. You can easily test the device by dropping a robust substitute for eggs into the bowl. The sensitivity of the device is easily controlled by varying the thickness of the foam layer or by using a different material which is more, or less, rigid.

The results with this system can be surprisingly good and there are many fast moving subjects you can try to capture on film. For example, if you tether an inflated balloon on top of the trigger platform, a dart dropping on to it can create sufficient pressure to fire the flash, if you adjust the system to the limit of its sensitivity. Alternatively, the

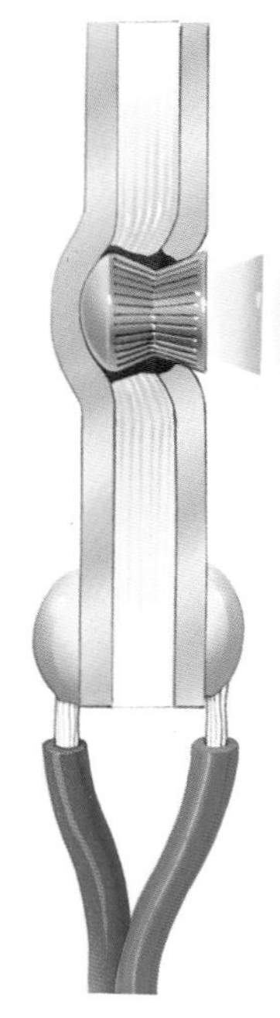

Caught and shot *To photograph a pellet hitting a metal plate, a target is made from two thin plates acting as the flash contacts. When the pellet hits the target it either passes through, and so completes the flash circuit, or buckles the plates so that they touch. By having the flash unit close to the target the output needed is reduced, giving a shorter flash duration*

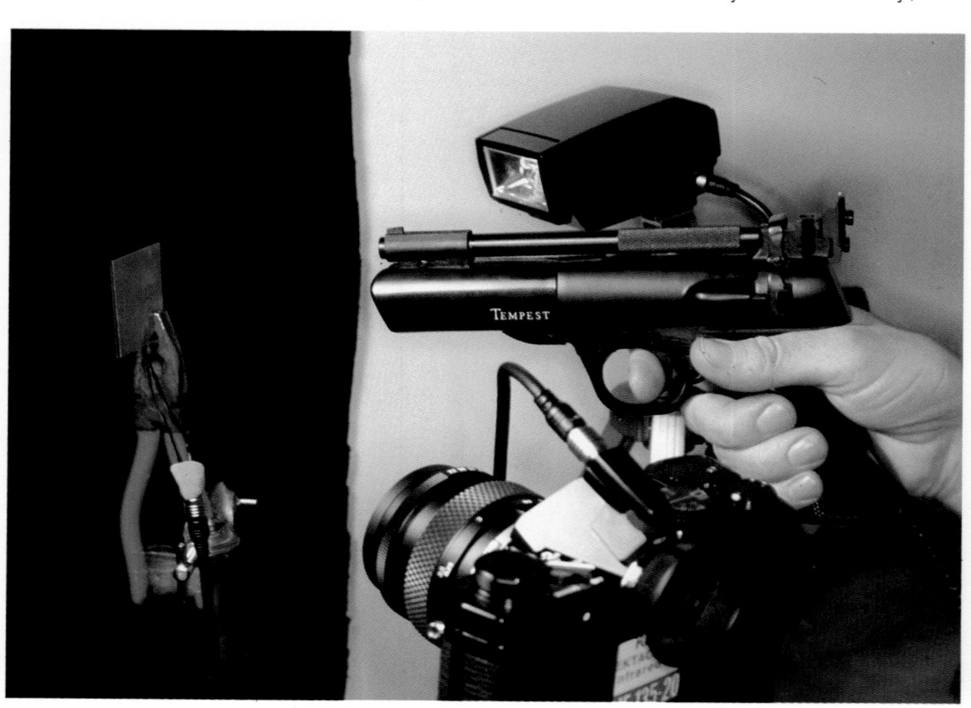

Bursting balloons *These balloons are at different stages of being burst by a pellet and show how the flash synchronization affects the object's appearance*

whole apparatus can be stood on its side, to photograph a fist pounding into a punchball. However, for many subjects, such as arrows or airgun pellets, impact triggering is inadequate. Although some people use sophisticated electronic methods, you can still improvise a fairly simple trigger providing you do not mind it appearing in the picture.

For example, to photograph an airgun pellet passing through a thin sheet of metal you can use a sandwich made up of two thinner sheets, separated by an equally thin layer of an insulating material in the corners of the sheets. Use paper or thin plastic sheet of the type used in scale models for the insulation. Each conducting metal layer is connected to one of the flash lead wires, and when the pellet passes through the target, the two outer layers are briefly connected by the metal pellet and the flash fires. Alternatively, the flash may be fired by the plates buckling and so coming into contact with each other.

Making the exposure

As with any other picture, attention to detail and careful photographic technique are essential in high-speed photography. If you are using projectiles such as darts or airgun pellets, keep the camera well away from the action and make sure there is something to absorb the flying object—such as a sandbag or a solid piece of wood. Remember that, for exposure determination, it is the distance from the subject to the flash, not the camera, that counts. Set the camera up on a tripod, and accurately line up all parts of the subject before focusing the camera. You may want to use a telephoto lens if camera and subject are kept well apart for safety reasons. Darts, falling eggs and bullets always travel in predictable paths, so you should have little difficulty deciding where to focus. If the flash has a choice of power outputs, set it to the lowest power—that is to say, the widest aperture—as this gives the shortest possible flash duration. Pay attention to the instructions packed with your particular flashgun, because there will almost certainly be a minimum distance specified. If the flashgun and subject are too close, your pictures will be overexposed.

Read off the required aperture for the film speed you are using from the scale on the flashgun, and make a series of test exposures. You can do this on black and white film, so that you can make an on-the-spot check on exposure before shooting in colour. This black and white test film needs only to be developed and quickly fixed before it is used for exposure evaluation—washing, drying and printing are unnecessary. If you have a flashmeter, or a camera which can be used with Polaroid film, these provide even better exposure checks.

Even after an exposure check, you should still take care to bracket your pictures at one, or half stop intervals over a two stop range, because of the effects of reciprocity failure (see panel).

Sophisticated triggers

It is not always possible for the subject of a high-speed flash picture to trigger the exposure directly, and a number of indirect triggering methods are commonly used. One of these is a *sound trigger*, which fires the flash when there is a loud noise. This system is ideal for photographing flying bullets, for example, because the noise from the muzzle of the gun can be used to fire the flash. A microphone is used to pick up the sound, and a special circuit closes the flash contacts after a short delay. The length of the delay—and the distance that the bullet flies before the flash fires—is varied by changing the distance between microphone and the gun.

Sound triggers of this type are sometimes available in shops, but they can be built quite easily by someone who has experience of electronic circuit design and construction.

Another convenient way to fire the flash is to arrange for the subject to break a beam of infrared radiation which lies in its path. This technique is particularly suitable for wildlife photography, where the exact path and direction of the subject cannot be accurate predicted. Many infrared triggers are now on the market and are generally easy to use. The problems lie in positioning the unit.

Reciprocity failure

When exposures are very short, film does not behave as you would expect it to, and a phenomenon known as reciprocity failure becomes a problem. This is more often encountered when exposures are very long, and affects colour film particularly.

In practice, reciprocity failure leads to underexposure when you use an automatic flashgun at short distances. To compensate, you should open up the lens aperture slightly more than the chart on the flashgun suggests, and if your camera is loaded with colour film, you may also have to use a colour correction filter.

The exact amount of extra exposure varies from film to film—for example, at an exposure time of 1/10,000 second, Ektachrome 200 film needs an extra half stop. Colour correction depends on both film and flashgun, and can only be exactly determined by trial and error, although a good starting point is to use 10 units of yellow filtration over the flashgun or lens.

Chapter 5

LIGHT INDOORS
Available light

Mixed lighting *Deliberately adding a tungsten light to the window light has produced a more atmospheric portrait*

The available light you find indoors cannot be controlled in the way that flashguns and other lighting equipment can and calls for the use of different techniques. Without being able to alter the strength, direction or nature of the light being used, the photographer has to learn to make best use of what is already there.

Available light, sometimes called existing light, refers to the normal lighting which you find in a room. In daylight, this would mean the natural light coming through the windows and perhaps supplemented with some artificial lighting. It may also mean a small amount of daylight with artificial light as the main illumination. At night, the available light will consist solely of artificial lighting although this itself may consist of a mixture of different types such as tungsten bulbs and fluorescent tubes.

Many people think that taking photographs indoors without special lighting equipment inevitably leads to poor results. This should not be the case and, although there are problems coping with the variations of available light, the results are often more natural than the harsh effects often created by a flashgun.

Contrast problems

One of the difficulties associated with using available light indoors is the inherent contrast of the light source itself. This is usually daylight coming through a window which produces hard side light, but it can also be domestic lamps. Daylight outside, on the other hand, is always much more soft because of the influence of skylight and the effect of clouds, nearby buildings and walls.

Exposures indoors will normally be rather long with slow or medium speed films so that, on the whole, it makes more sense to use fast films such as Tri-X or HP5 (400 ASA/ISO) for black and white. For colour transparencies use films such as Ektachrome 400—though in certain circumstances it may be better to use slower, tungsten-balanced film (page 81). These higher speed films will allow you to use shorter exposures to freeze movement or increase depth of field. Fast films are inherently less contrasty than slower

Natural light *The mood created by natural light can influence the whole shot. A tripod is needed in low light*

ones and this has the advantage of helping to counter the problem of increased contrast indoors.

One further advantage of using fast films is that they can be *uprated.* Most black and white and colour transparency film with speeds of 400 ASA can be uprated to 1600 ASA quite safely where it would have been either impossible or inconvenient to use the film at its recommended speed. Suppose, for instance, your exposure meter gave a reading of 1/8 second at *f*/2 for a shot indoors at 400 ASA. By uprating the film to 1600 ASA you could use 1/30 second at *f*/2 which would allow you to hand hold the camera whereas with the former setting you would have to use a tripod to eliminate camera shake. Do not forget that if you uprate films an adjustment in the processing will have to be made.

Unless the room in which you are shooting is white or lightly coloured, the lighting contrast is likely to be very great. For this reason it is important to position the subject carefully in relation to the light source. There will probably be several stops difference between the highlight areas adjacent to the light source and the shadow areas in the background. This calls for very accurate and intelligent use of the exposure meter. It is usually better to take light readings off the relevant portion of the main subject. If necessary you can use a reflector, which need be nothing more elaborate than a piece of white card, paper or sheet to fill in shadow detail. Obviously large areas to be filled in will need either a large reflector or an additional light source.

It is very important to realize that low levels of illumination, such as from a 80 watt bulb, do not necessarily mean soft light. On the contrary, most domestic lighting is very contrasty because its position high up on the wall or ceiling throws big, harsh shadows.

Assessing lighting contrast and deciding whether what you see through the viewfinder of your camera will actually be recorded by the film is perhaps the single most important aspect of photography. Modern film, whether colour or black and white, is unable to cope with the same brightness or contrast range as the human eye. This means that what your eye sees in a particular scene will not necessarily be recorded in its entirety on the final negative or transparency. There is a very simple trick which artists have traditionally used to evaluate the shape and contrast of their subjects. This is to squint at your subject—to close your eyes so that you can just see a dim outline of the scene in front of you. Note that the shadow and highlight areas which contain detail with your eyes fully open now no longer register. The film will react in a very similar fashion.

Once you get used to using this discipline every time you view a difficult shot you will avoid disappointing results where what you saw in the first place does not appear in the photograph.

There are occasions, particularly with architectural interiors, when you want not only to record detail in the deep shadow areas but also to highlight detail such as bright daylight streaming through a window. With normal average exposure readings and film development, only the mid tone areas will record any significant detail. The highlights will be burned out while the shadow areas will go black. There is not much to be done in this kind of situation with colour materials, short of using supplementary fill-in lighting. But with black and white film over which you have development control you can 'compress' the tonal range of the film. The secret is to expose for the shadows and develop for the highlights. Normally this technique is used with large format cameras where single sheets of film can be exposed and developed individually to give the exact effect required but there is no reason why the same technique cannot be applied to 35 mm format, as long as you treat the rest of the film this way.

Using window light

To get used to available light, begin by taking portraits or simple still life arrangements just using the daylight coming through a window. A variety of

Railway coach *Although these tungsten lamps have made the colours artificially warm, this shot is still attractive*

effects can be treated in this way by moving your subject experimentally in relation to the window light. You can light from the front by positioning your subject face-on to the window and taking the photograph from outside facing in. Alternatively, use sidelighting so that half the face is brightly lit while the other side is in deep shadow. A silhouette can be achieved by shooting directly into the window with your subject facing you. The variations are endless, especially if you use a white reflector to fill in the shadow detail.

Watch very carefully for background detail such as bookshelves and standard lamps interfering with your subject; because of the great difference in contrast between the foreground and background you may not be aware of obtrusive detail. Exposure readings also have to be very carefully evaluated in view of the enormous range of brightness levels.

Even with fast film, when you are using available daylight indoors, you will usually have to use fairly slow shutter speeds—1/60 or slower—if your aperture is to be anything but wide open. To avoid camera shake, especially with longer focal length lenses, you will need to support the camera in some way. A sturdy tripod is ideal but a table top with a pile of books for final height adjustment will suffice with care. A tripod is also a very useful disciplining element in that it makes you much more decisive about the framing and positioning of your final shot. Use a cable release, or the camera's self-timer, to fire the shutter without vibration.

Blacksmith *In pictures like this the light itself is the strongest point. A flashgun would have spoilt the mood*

Colour balance

The quality of daylight varies considerably according to the time of day and the season of the year. Winter sunlight, where the sun is low and casts long shadows, is entirely different from summer sunlight, where the sun is high in the sky and casts short shadows.

This clearly makes a considerable difference to the amount of light available. While the winter sun is generally weaker, it may actually illuminate a south facing room more because more direct light comes through the window.

The colour temperature of daylight also varies according to the time of day and prevailing weather conditions. An obvious instance is red sunset light compared to the bluishness of a cloudy, rainy day. Although it is fairly easy to assess the quality and colour temperature of daylight outdoors, it becomes more difficult indoors since there are other factors which influence it. The colour of walls, floors, carpets and curtains can influence the final colour of the film. Windows themselves can diffuse light or concentrate it depending on the angle of light and the optical quality of the glass.

Shooting with black and white material obviously eliminates many of these problems since there is no colour to worry about—the main factor, apart

Finnish gypsies *The warm tones in this shot are caused by an overhead tungsten bulb which supplemented the daylight*

mixed lighting, try and increase one single source of lighting to produce a more dominant type of light. This will help you to decide which film to use and you may find that all you have to do is open the curtains more fully or add an extra reading lamp or reflector.

Conversion filters

Another method of balancing colour film to different light sources is to use various colour balancing filters over the camera lens.

Two of the most useful filters are those numbered 80A and 85B. The 80A is a blue filter for exposing daylight colour film in tungsten illumination. The 85B is an amber filter which is used for exposing tungsten balanced film in daylight. Both of these filters cut down the amount of light reaching the film and you need to increase the exposure by 2 stops for the 80A and about 2/3 stops for the 85B.

from composition and lighting, is being able to cope with contrast.

Apart from daylight, which is the commonest photographic light source there are other manmade light sources which are used indoors when there is little or no daylight to make short enough exposures.

Since different light sources emit various colour temperatures, it is highly probable that if you take pictures by available light you will encounter one of the photographer's nightmares—mixed lighting. When taking a simple shot of a living room and kitchen interior, for example, you are likely to have a mixture of daylight, tungsten and fluorescent lighting, all of which would produce different colour casts.

What you have to establish before all else is the dominant light source. This can be done by roughly assessing the lighting ratio by eye. Turn the artificial lights off and stand back to see what difference this makes to the shadow detail if there is a lot of daylight streaming through the doors or windows. Alternatively, use an exposure meter to measure the relative brightness. Do this by taking a reading from the areas lit by daylight and another from the tungsten lit areas. Use the appropriate colour film for the light source which is strongest.

If the room in which you are photographing has a fairly equal mix of daylight and tungsten light the decision is more difficult. If you use daylight type colour film to record the daylight parts of the picture accurately, the tungsten lit portions will have a warm reddish cast over them. If on the other hand you decide to use tungsten type film then the daylight portions of the pictures will go cold and bluish. Pictures with a warmish cast are generally far more acceptable than ones with a cold bluish cast so that it is usual, if in any real doubt as to what film to use, to shoot with daylight type colour film.

When you run into problems with

Still life *Backlighting from a window can be used effectively for a wide range of still life shots*

Cat and rabbit *A window gives a diffuse and natural illumination which can be ideal lighting for portraits*

Shooting interiors

Shooting any subject indoors can be awkward enough, but making a photograph of the interior itself can tax the ingenuity of the photographer to its limits. The problem is to capture all the colour and detail in the interior without losing its atmosphere. Often the available light, from windows and electric lights, is far from adequate for photography. Or it may be far too contrasty—the difference in brightness between a south-facing window and a dark corner is massive. Yet introducing fill-in lighting could destroy the atmosphere. The key to success lies in careful juggling of available light and added light.

Shooting by available light

Some scenes are lit perfectly adequately and evenly by the available light. Even if the light is not sufficient for a hand-held shot, you can often get good results by using a long exposure on a tripod, without resorting to additional lighting. Careful placing of the camera, particularly keeping windows out of the shot, can help to avoid excessive contrast ratios. This technique often gives very natural looking results because you use only the rooms normal lighting.

There are a few precautions to taken when using the long exposures needed for this technique. The main concern is the exposure iteself, and the problem of reciprocity failure. Most films are manufactured with an optimum exposure time, and the film speed is calculated at that exposure time.

Reciprocity failure is particularly likely with daylight films. For most daylight films, the manufacturers expect the film to be exposed at about 1/125

The drawing room *was shot using both flash and available light—daylight and room lights. Eight exposures were made on the same sheet of film, with the room lights left on for five of them.*
Church light *The large windows and light interior allowed the church to be shot by available daylight alone*

Daylight only *With just the light coming through the windows, the room looks fairly attractive. But there are many areas, such as the far corner, where detail is hidden in shadow*

Colour cast *With very long exposures, the picture can have a cast due to reciprocity failure. Here a 15 second exposure was made on Ektachrome 200, giving a very green picture*

second. When the exposure times are much longer, the film becomes less efficient at recording light and its colour balance changes. To gain an accurate and well-exposed result with extended exposures, filtration may be needed (see page 103).

Because of the high risk of reciprocity failure with daylight films, it is often better to shoot on tungsten film even when the available light is natural daylight. Tungsten films are designed for studio use, and are therefore more suitable for long exposures—manufacturers expect exposures in the order of ½ second. But when they are used in an interior lit by daylight, the emulsion has to be converted to daylight use with an 85B filter.

One of the big problems with shooting interiors on colour film is colour balance. With daylight alone, an 85B filter with tungsten film is quite adequate. But when artificial light sources are included, the problems are more complex.

Many large interiors have built-in floodlighting which provides excellent illumination, provided you can tell the colour temperature of the lights used. Tungsten halogen lighting is commonly fitted to interiors like cathedrals and here it is advisable to shoot on tungsten film. The floodlighting is often rather lower in colour temperature than the 3200K for which tungsten film is balanced and this gives a reddish result unless some blue filtration is used.

For really critical colour rendering, a colour temperature meter will tell you what colour the lights are burning at, and some even tell you what filtration to use.

Fluorescent tubes pose a particular problem, as their colour temperature varies from type to type (daylight, warmlight and so on) and changes with age. Some colour meters will give colour temperature readings for fluorescent tubes, but these are rare. However, if you know the make and type of tube, tables provided by Kodak will suggest a filtration. As a starting point some filter manufacturers supply filters for converting fluorescent to daylight—but it is wise to do a test if the results are critical.

Mixed lighting is even harder to cope with and it is best to avoid it if possible. If you are shooting in tungsten light, for instance, pull the curtains over the windows or wait till darkness. Alternatively, frame to exclude windows from the shot altogether.

Establishing the exposure

Whatever type of lighting you are faced with, and whatever film you are using, it is sensible to bracket the shots by at least one and a half stops either side of the meter reading. There are so many variables with these types of shot that it is often difficult to gauge the exposure accurately. When taking the meter reading, take care to keep any bright windows out of the view of the meter, as these will distort the reading. Aim instead at the floor, or some mid toned area within the shot. If your meter can read incident light, a reading from the centre of the room, pointing towards the

Available lighting *Switching the room lights on gives an improvement on daylight alone, though it is still not ideal. A 10R red filter was used to compensate for slight reciprocity failure*

Just flash *Four flash units were used in all—three at the far end of the room, to the right of the camera, and a snooted one on the left. This shot shows how the flash contributes to the main shot*

camera may be extremely useful.

As a starting point for bracketing, it is common practice to take an incident light reading, then a reflected reading from the floor, and split the difference. A spot meter is useful for measuring the range of contrast between the brightest and the darkest areas. If you do not have a spot meter and your camera has TTL metering, you can use your camera as a spot meter by fitting the longest lens you have. If the meter tells you that the brightest point needs an exposure of 1 second at f/16, and the darkest area is 1 minute at f/16, then you have a range of seven stops to cope with, which is outside the range of many films. For a satisfactory exposure you need to throw some light into the darkest areas and bring them up to within about four stops of the highlights.

Using flash

A great deal can be achieved with hand-held flash guns. Unfortunately, however, a single flash usually lacks sufficient power, so a system of multiple flashes is called for.

With a typical subject—a room with coloured walls, a white ceiling, a dark carpet and a dark sofa along one wall opposite the windows—an incident light reading, taken in the middle of the room, might give an exposure of eight seconds at f/11. Spot readings tell you that the areas nearest the windows need two seconds at f/11. If the exposure is made according to the incident reading, the lighter areas will be highlit, but not bleached out. The readings for the sofa and carpet indicate three minutes at f/11, which is more than three stops below the general reading. If the available light is not supplemented, shadow areas will lack detail, so the floor and sofa need additional light. With hand-held flashguns this seems impossible—the sofa is three metres away, but at three metres your flashgun will only yield an exposure of f/4. What you need is f/8—one stop less than the incident reading. By keeping the level of fill-in flash about one stop less than the general incident reading, the result will be more natural.

To get your flashgun to yield an exposure of f/8, you need to get four flashes out of it (one flash gives f/4: two flashes give f/5.6: four flashes give f/8). But your flashgun takes ten seconds or more to recycle so four flashes would take 30 seconds, almost four times as long as the total exposure indicated by the incident reading.

The simplest solution is to make a multiple exposure, using one exposure for each flash. Unfortunately, most cameras do not have a suitable multiple exposure facility. The answer to this problem is to cover the lens while the flashgun is recycling. For this you need a piece of black card, as matt as possible, which you simply hold in front of the lens during the recycling process. So to take the photograph in the example above, you cover the lens with the card, open the shutter on the B setting, remove the card and immediately fire the flash, then quickly cover the lens again. When the flash has recycled, you repeat the procedure.

After four flashes you have built up the fill-in lighting, and you can give the film its time exposure. A stable tripod will help to prevent the camera being jogged as the card is moved in and out of place.

If you have more than one flashgun, you can place your extra guns where they will lighten up dark corners. Position them carefully and if possible trigger them with slave units so that no flashguns or cables appear in the frame.

To avoid harsh shadows from the gun nearest the camera, you can move it around slightly from one flash to the next.

All photographs by Angelo Hornak

Best combination *As there was daylight coming through the windows, daylight film was used, with tungsten lights converted to daylight using blue filters*

An umbrella reflector on each gun will soften the results even more—but will also reduce the power of the flash and, unless you have a flash meter, brollies make it difficult to assess the output. The disadvantages of this system are that your arms begin to ache holding the card still in front of the lens and, more seriously, the overall lighting effect cannot be seen at the time you are taking the shot. One of the flashguns, for instance, might be reflecting in a mirror.

To control the flash lighting properly, you really need professional studio flash heads with modelling lights. Unfortunately these are expensive and considerably bulkier than flashguns. But they have a higher output, allowing the use of diffusers and umbrellas, and they recycle faster, usually within a second or two. However, even with studio flash heads it is usually necessary to give several flashes.

Fast shutters

On some occasions you need fast shutter speeds and several flashes—for example, where you are taking an interior photograph where you also want to record the view out of a window.

Take a case where the exposure for the outside view is 1/60 second at f/11. Your flash heads may give, say, f/5.6 for one flash, but f/5.6 does not give you enough depth of field, and you really need to use f/11. To get to f/11 you need four flashes: but you can not cover and uncover the lens with black card fast enough—with this technique the exterior will be hopelessly over-exposed. One answer is to take four exposures of 1/250 second each at f/11, with the flash firing each time.

Flash fill *With no additional lighting, windows have too large a brightness range to record on film without losing detail (far left). Using flash allows you to expose for the outside scene and still show interior details of the room*

Too orange *This is similar to the previous shot, but without converting the lamps to daylight, resulting in an orange cast on the parts lit by tungsten*

Too blue *Switching to tungsten film gives the correct balance for the lights. But those areas lit by the daylight are far too blue*

Just lights *By excluding the daylight the scene is lit by the unfiltered lights alone. On tungsten film this gives correct colour rendering*

A shutter synchronized at 1/250 second is needed. Unfortunately, few 35 mm cameras have this facility—which is one of the reasons why professionals tend to do this sort of work on larger formats.

You also need to be able to recock the shutter without advancing the film, or jogging the camera. Large format cameras have lenses with their own shutters which are fully synchronized, and it is possible with care to recock the shutter by hand without jogging the camera. But it is safer to use a shutter like the Prontor Press which is self-cocking via a cable release.

An alternative method is to rig up a remote controlled servo motor to recock the shutter and to fire it from across a room, or even from the other end of a cathedral. This system has the advantage that the photographer can move the lights around between flashes, without going near the camera.

Balancing the light

Even with modelling lights it is hard to be certain what the balance between the daylight and the flash heads is going to be. A Polaroid back is invaluable for checking the lighting ratios.

Often there are light fittings, such as chandeliers, which are part of the decoration and should be illuminated. But if they are on for all the exposures they would be overexposed. The solution is to leave them switched on for only half the total exposure.

In exceptional cases where a really massive flash output is needed—in photographing a cathedral nave with a dark roof, for example—blue flashbulbs can be used. A special unit can fire up to four bulbs at once. The bulbs themselves are comparatively expensive and have to be changed for each shot, making bracketing time consuming and costly. But they have the advantage of being lightweight, with a high output, and they are independent of the mains supply. Individual bulbs can be fired with slave units, and very complicated lighting set ups are possible but this approach means carrying many bulbs around.

Using tungsten lighting

Flash lighting is invaluable for colour work because its colour balance matches any daylight coming into the scene. But if you are working in black and white this is no longer a consideration, and any type of lighting can be used. It is best to avoid negatives that are too contrasty, so with black and white it is advisable to overexpose and underdevelop the film. Tungsten lighting has several advantages over flash—it is cheaper and lighter, you do not need a special flash meter, and you get what you see. This is particularly useful for avoiding reflections in mirrors, picture frames, or even just glossy paintwork.

There are various types of tungsten lighting suitable for interiors, from photofloods in inexpensive reflectors to high intensity quartz iodine or tungsten halogen lights. With all these types, diffusers can be used in front of the light.

Tungsten lights can be converted to daylight for use with colour materials, but there is a big loss of output. Blue gelatin filters, or a blue reflector can be used: and some lighting equipment manufacturers supply glass dichroic filters, which are heat resistant. If tungsten lighting has to be used, and it is not practical to convert it to daylight, then it may be possible to exclude any daylight from the shot, and work entirely on tungsten film. You may even have to wait until dark for some shots.

Radio City *To keep the atmosphere of the place, tungsten lamps were used as the main light source, so that they matched the available room lighting*

Chapter 6

CONTROLLED LIGHT
Portable studio

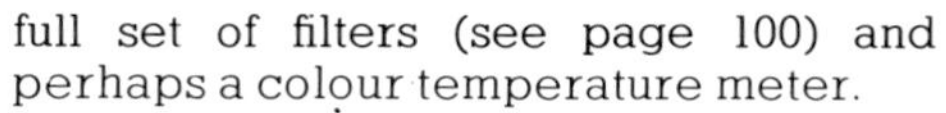

There is usually a distinct difference between a photograph taken in a studio and one taken on location. Both amateurs and professionals regard studio quality as the utmost of which their equipment is capable, but often expect quality to suffer once they are in unfamiliar territory. Yet there are ways of creating studio conditions in even the least promising surroundings.

You might, for example, wish to photograph some interesting object which you discover while on holiday, far from home—a fossil embedded in rocks, a work of art or even an example of local cratsmanship, perhaps. You may be interested in taking photographs of particular objects as part of your hobby, from car badges to antiquities. In each case, the simple snapshot probably will not be adequate, and you will wish that you had better facilities at your disposal.

But if you are prepared to take care over your photography when you are away from home, there is a great deal you can do to improve matters, and even to produce results of studio quality. The main restriction is that you simply cannot carry all the lights and backgrounds that you normally associate with studio work. Even so you can get by with surprisingly little additional load.

Intense shots *These shots were taken on location in Tibet using tent lighting. The Guru (left) was lit with available window light plus reflectors. The skull bowl (above) suffers from lack of depth of field as small flashguns were used*

The camera and accessories

Although most amateurs automatically expect to use their regular camera, it is worth considering how a professional would approach the problem of taking studio quality pictures on location, maybe in a remote part of the world where service facilities and even simple items are hard or impossible to obtain. The ideal would be a roll film camera with a wide range of facilities, such as camera movements and interchangeable lenses. Some cameras, such as the Linhof Technica 70, offer this. Alternatively, a reliable roll film camera with more restricted facilities, such as a Hasselblad, could be used. If both these were out of the question, a professional might use a top quality 35 mm camera with a range of lenses, including shift and macro lenses.

But whatever the camera, it is important that the shutter should be completely mechanical, using no batteries, or offer manual speeds if the batteries fail. Though batteries are widely available, and you can take spares, they can sometimes let you down at the worst possible moment, and your spares may also turn out to be faulty. Few professionals would feel happy at relying solely on an electronically controlled shutter when at a remote location. Other essentials would be a light meter—again, one using no batteries such as the Weston Master, a full set of filters (see page 100) and perhaps a colour temperature meter.

A tripod and cable release are essential. The tripod should be as sturdy as you can bear to carry—a flimsy one is worse than useless.

It is always worth using a viewfinder magnifier when working with 35 mm. This makes focusing much more precise, which is important if you want high quality results.

Backgrounds and lighting

While the equipment you carry must largely depend on what you regularly use and have available, the main problems with attempting studio work on location involve the backgrounds and the lighting.

Large quantities of background paper are obviously not practical, and even small quantities will soon become creased, dirty and useless. Whenever possible, you should use 'natural' backgrounds, and improvise where necessary. This applies particularly to portraits, where it is thoroughly impractical to carry a sufficient area of paper to make any difference. There are, however, two other possibilities.

The first is black velvet. A piece a metre or a metre and a half square will fold down to a very compact bundle, and may be shaken out adequately flat to be used as a backdrop to any local artefacts—pots, knives, small statues, works of art and so on. Because it is such an efficient absorber of light, black velvet simply will not show up in a colour transparency where the subject is correctly exposed. This makes the subject appear to float in space, which can be very effective. The only drawback is that it can become monotonous.

The second possibility is locally obtained fabrics. This is especially true in India, where light cottons in a wide variety of colours are obtainable very cheaply. 'Double width' (two metre) fabric can be used either reasonably smooth, or gathered to give the effect of drapes. Heavier fabrics can be used in the same way as the black velvet to give a little variety.

Unless the background is important, or

Softer light *Quartz lighting is useful but can give hard shadows (left). Putting a diffuser in front of the lamp (below) gives softer lighting (right)*

unless the subject is actually resting on it, the best approach is often to use a wide aperture and selective focus so that it is not very clear. Provided there are no violently contrasting patches of colour or brightness, this should not be obvious.

Lighting is even more of a problem. Ideally, you should work with available light whenever possible. This makes no demands on erratic power supplies or heavy, expensive and irreplaceable batteries, but it is also unpredictable in colour, quantity, and harshness.

Each of these variables is, however, controllable. The first, colour, is only important if you are using transparency film, and can usually be corrected with filtration: this is where the colour temperature meter comes in. It cannot easily be corrected, however, if it is changing quickly (for example, at sunset) or if it derives from fluorescent tubes, as in a museum or other building. Evening light can add character to a shot as it becomes redder, but fluorescent lighting (or worse still mixed lighting) is disastrous: a CC20M filter, an FL-D filter or an FL-W filter may improve fluorescent lighting, but the results will still be unpredictable and possibly unusable. The only real possibilities are moving the subject, turning off the fluorescents and working by daylight, or adding artificial light, such as flash.

Indoors, it may be possible to increase the amount of light simply by opening curtains and doors. You may increase the lighting by several stops in this way. It may also be possible to shoot at another time, when the sun is shining from a different direction. But if the light is simply coming from the wrong direction then reflectors are needed.

Reflectors can be as simple as a sheet of newspaper or a piece of white cloth—even a T-shirt will often make a significant difference—or they may be purpose-made. Three of the most useful possibilities for studio photography on location are: aluminium foil, crumpled and then smoothed out before being stuck on a piece of cardboard or packing case (the crumbling helps prevent 'hot spots' in the reflected light); white fabric stretched over light wooden frameworks (use bought laths or bamboos, or even wood cut from trees); and purpose-made reflectors, such as the Lastolite.

Plain white or textured silver reflectors do not alter the colour of the light—the main difference is that textured silver reflectors are more efficient. Some people use gold coloured reflectors for flattering skin tones.

The plain white reflectors can also be used as diffusers to modify harsh, directional light: a typical diffuser might reflect 50 per cent of the light falling on it and diffuse the other 50 per cent through it. Once again alternatives include large pieces of white cloth. These can be pinned in a window, like curtains. There is also the possibility of using a black Lastolite, or something similar, to shade the subject or to prevent reflections from nearby surfaces.

Useful accessories ***Above are the best types of reflector—foil, umbrella and Lastolite (which folds to the size of the small blue bag). The bracket (right) allows you to fit a flashgun to a tripod, for easier and more versatile lighting***

There comes a point, however, where there is simply not enough light, and reflectors and diffusers are of no use. Very long exposure times should be avoided because of *reciprocity failure* (see page 103). At this juncture, you are forced back on additional lighting. Simple on-camera flash is extremely unlikely to be able to deliver the effects you want, so multiple flash will be needed. An alternative, if the power is reliable and if you can totally exclude other light, is tungsten lighting—preferably tungsten halogen—with plenty of spare bulbs. But this involves carrying a considerable extra load.

The best form of additional lighting is therefore flash. A good set-up will include a large powerful gun, preferably with switchable power, and anything up to half a dozen small guns with slave units. These can be quite inexpensive, costing less than a couple of rolls of transparency film each. With just one extension lead for the big gun, you have a main light source with plenty of fill-in; you can also group the small guns together for greater intensity.

You should make sure if possible that all the guns run on the same size of batteries—the AA pencil-cell size is fairly universal and is easy to carry. An excellent idea is to carry rechargeable (NiCd) batteries, if there is any chance of being able to recharge them. A well-planned expedition will use AA batteries for everything.

To hold small flashguns in place, use

tape or putty-type adhesive. Lightweight tripods can also come in handy, offering you good control over positioning. If you use a tripod, buy the adapters sold for attaching flashguns to lighting stands, which have a tripod screw fitting insert.

A flash meter is also essential, though it is a bad idea to rely on it totally, particularly because you will need a battery to run it. In practice, a Polaroid test is almost the only way to be sure of high quality, professional results, but this means you must use a roll film camera with a Polaroid back.

A Polaroid test allows you to check both the effect of the flashguns and the exposure, which you scale up or down according to the speed of the film you are using. It is also true that errors, things left in shot and so on, show up more clearly in a Polaroid than in real life. Even with a Polaroid test, bracketing of exposures is advisable; without a Polaroid, it is essential.

Unduly harsh flash lighting can be softened with reflectors and diffusers, as already described, but for shadowless lighting of small objects (up to, say, 60 cm high), a *tent* is useful. This is no more than a lightweight framework covered in thin white cloth, inside which the subject is placed. Black velvet provides a background, while the top, sides, and front (with a hole cut for the camera lens) diffuse and reflect the light. If you are staying in one place for some time, you can have one made up by the local carpenter, or you can lash one together yourself from sticks and gaffer tape. Some people even take collapsible frames of aluminium. The easiest shape to make, and to work with, is a cube—but if you have two, or better still, three light tripods you can make an excellent tent with these.

The easiest approach is to set up one tripod with a transverse pole which holds the velvet as a backdrop. The second tripod forms an 'A' at the other end, with its third leg extended and gaffer-taped to the tip of the first. With white cloth draped over the whole assembly, and held in place with clips or clamps, the result is a very useful tent.

The result is ideal for photographing small objects under diffuse lighting—you can either use daylight or flash. Even if you shine the flash from one side only the effect of the tent will be to make it quite non-directional. If you are photographing a shiny object it might be neccessary to make sure that the inner framework is completely covered by the white cloth.

Even white cloth can have a slight coloration, so if you are using transparency film you should do a trial run if possible. You may find that an 82 series blue filter will be needed to correct for a yellowish cast, though the bluish colour of flash or even a cloudy day might overcome the colour of the cloth.

But the most important factor in this kind of work is meticulous attention to detail—and for this you need patience.

Setting up a tent

The best material for the frame is thin wood or bamboo which can be either taped or nailed together

Place the object you want to photograph on a suitable background, and then cover the frame with white cloth

After setting up the camera, preferably on a tripod, cover the front of the tent with cloth, making a hole for the lens

Use a hand-held meter, rather than the camera's built-in one. The best way of metering is the incident light method

With some types of cloth, especially if it is fairly thick, you will find that the shot has a slight yellow cast

If the light in the tent is too yellow, use an 82 filter to correct. If in doubt, shoot pictures with and without the filter

Chapter 7

SLIDE CRAFT
Slide copying

Copying quality *Even in a good copy, there is inevitably a slight, but acceptable loss of colour, highlight detail and definition from the original (left) but in a copy made from a copy (above), loss of quality can be severe*

There are many reasons why copies or duplicates of original transparencies are needed. Unlike negatives, which are only an intermediate stage between the taking of a photograph and the final print, a transparency is a one-of-a-kind original. Lose it, and you lose the only record you have of the original scene. A duplicate of the original, however, can be used regularly without fear.

As well as making straightforward facsimilies or true copies of an original, you can also make modifications during the duplicating process, to correct for slight faults such as colour casts or underexposure. And by copying more than one original on to the same piece of film, you can create new images altogether. Such images can be made in the camera on location, but when using a duplicator you can experiment, and can call upon your entire library of images (see pages 85 to 89). There is inevitably a slight loss in quality compared with in-camera effects, but the advantages are considerable.

The additional equipment you may need for making your own duplicates can range from none at all, if you have your own slide projector, through an inexpensive slide copier, to a professional quality bench copier which will cost considerably more than the average SLR camera. The quality obtainable increases with the amount of equipment, but for comparatively little outlay it is possible to get very satisfactory results.

Using a projector

Since most photographers who use slide film own a projector, this method of copying original slides is very economical. It involves projecting the slide and photographing the projected image.

When setting up your equipment for copying by projection, it is very important to realize that the surface on to which the original is being projected affects the quality of the copy more than any other factor. The copying camera must be mounted on a tripod as close as possible to the axis of the projector lens, and should be aligned so that it is pointing directly at the screen surface. The screen should be as plain and flat as possible.

Since nearly all modern projectors are equipped with tungsten halogen light sources with a colour temperature of about 3200 K, tungsten balanced film is usually best for duplicates. If possible, avoid using daylight film with a conversion filter (normally the blue 80A) as this would add nearly two *f*-stops to the exposure which will aggravate the problems of focus and camera shake.

For the best quality use the minimum practicable projected enlargement, which will therefore give the brightest possible image.

The exposure can be determined by either using the camera's through the lens exposure meter in the normal way, or by selecting an appropriate area in

Bench top copier *Sophisticated bench top units like this ensure good quality copies but are very expensive*

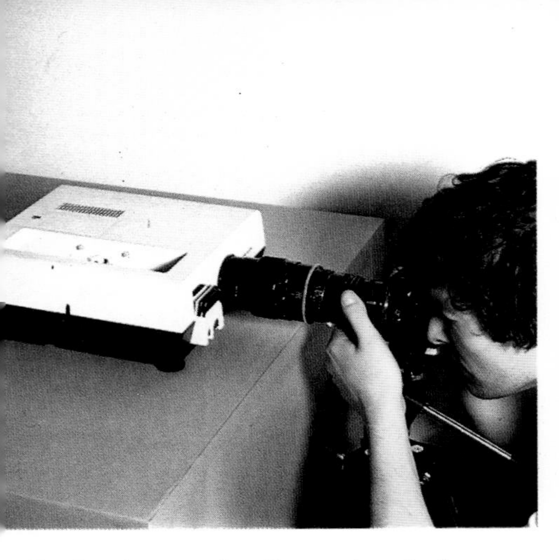

Projection copies *Removing the lens from a projector allows you to photograph the slide directly, using the projector itself as a light source*

Using a mirror *If you remove the lens from your camera, you can make good copies in the darkroom, using an enlarger and a front silvered mirror*

Minimum equipment *All you need for a rough and ready duplicate is your camera and enlarger, but this set-up needs very careful alignment*

the projected enlargement and measuring the light with a hand-held meter.

When estimating the exposure and taking the copy photograph, turn out all other lights in the room. It may also be a good idea to temporarily shield the light spilling from the lamp housing of the projector. But do not leave the shielding in place or the projector may overheat.

Framing the image in the viewfinder and focusing should be done very carefully. Remember that because most viewfinders show only the central 90 per cent of the actual image area, there is no need to allow for a border round the copy. Frame the projected image as tightly as possible. When you see the results you may even find that you can move in even closer.

The projection method can produce duplicates of fair quality. Its limitations are the fact that the image is being passed through both the projector lens and the camera lens; the quality of the screen; and the evenness of illumination of the projector, which may produce a 'hot spot' in the centre of the image.

If you have a set of extension tubes, you can avoid these problems by photographing the slide in the gate of the projector using the following technique.

Take the lens off the projector, and fit extension tubes to your camera. Use a telephoto lens if possible, since this allows a greater separation between lens and slide. Place the projector on a table, and set up the camera on a tripod, so that it looks into the aperture where the lens is normally fitted. Through the viewfinder of the camera, you will see a brilliantly illuminated image of the slide in the projector gate when you switch on the projector light.

In some slide projectors, the slide is deeply recessed within the body of the projector, and you may find it difficult to get the camera lens close enough to the slide. If you do have problems, try using a longer focal length lens, or even inserting the camera lens into the front of the projector.

Careful alignment of camera and projector is essential, and once it is correct, take great care not to disturb either camera or projector. If you have a motor winder, use this to avoid shaking the camera when you wind on, and always use a cable release on the camera. If your projector has a remote control use this to avoid moving the projector each time a slide is changed.

This way of copying slides is rather awkward to arrange, but once the position of camera and projector have been established, the process of copying is very fast. Using a motor winder, it need only take a minute or two to copy 36 slides.

Copies from your enlarger

If you own an enlarger, then you already have everything you need to produce high quality duplicate transparencies. The lens on an enlarger is ideal for use at short distances, and can give better copies than your camera lens. The light source in an enlarger also provides an even and consistent source of illumination for the transparency.

The simplest technique with an enlarger is to place the camera on the baseboard, and project the image of the slide into the camera body, without the camera lens. Unfortunately, it is difficult to view the image properly without a right angle viewfinder, and so some manufacturers make a front silvered mirror on a rigid bracket. This turns the path of the light from the enlarger through a right angle, and the camera can be used in a more normal position. The filter drawer of the enlarger can be used for colour correction, or a colour head can provide dial-in colour changes.

If the head on your enlarger turns to allow projection on to the wall, you may be able to fit your camera onto a tripod, and project the slide on to the film. This eliminates the need for any accessories.

Using a slide copier

There are a number of slide copiers on the market. The simplest consists of a close up lens in a barrel, with a holder for the transparency at one end. It is used in place of the camera lens, so it is completely self-contained.

The lens included in such devices may have a very small aperture—typically *f*/16—in order to give sharp images with good depth of field without using very costly optics. This means that the image may be so dim that a very bright light source is needed. One saving grace is that because the copier is firmly fixed to the camera, vibration is not much of a problem and time exposures are possible without much trouble.

Some versions have a zoom lens, enabling you to make selective enlarge-

Bellows copier *Selectively cropped copies can be made using a copier attachment fitted to a bellows unit*

Simple copier *Inexpensive copiers are capable of giving quite reasonable results and are easy to use*

Copying procedure *The first stage is to insert the slide into the copier—it fits behind a translucent plastic sheet which diffuses the illumination*

Focusing *A bright light source is needed, as simple copiers have a small aperture lens and the image in the viewfinder of the camera is very dim*

ments when copying.

Another device is intended to be used with a close-up bellows extension and the camera's own standard lens. The copier may have its own bellows, to allow for changing the scale of the image. The lens may be used with a close-up reversing ring to improve quality, and magnifications from 1 × to 10 × are possible. This camera–bellows–slide copier arrangement must be set up on a sturdy tripod, or preferably clamped to a bench, to eliminate camera shake. A cable release is essential.

Illumination

Whichever system you are using, there is a choice of light source. Daylight can be used, but it is not ideal because of its inconsistency in intensity and colour, unless you only need a quick, cheap reference duplicate.

For simplicity of operation, consistency and relatively low cost, tungsten is the light source that is usually preferred. The standard procedure is to place a tungsten photoflood 1 m or so directly behind the original in the slide holder. The light should not be any closer, or the slide may be damaged by the heat. If a tungsten photoflood is used with artificial light film, an 81A correction filter will be needed in order to correct for the slight difference in colour balance between light and film. It is best to use a gelatin filter placed between the light source and the transparency holder. In many cases, though, the small difference in colour balance can be ignored.

The exposure is easy to measure using the camera's TTL metering system (remembering that the 'stop-down' method has to be used once the lens is closed down since most units do not allow automatic stop-down metering).

With non-TTL metered cameras tests have to be made based on hand-held meter readings made by measuring the light transmitted through the transparency in its holder.

One other major advantage of using a tungsten light source in this way is the availability of low contrast duplicating film, balanced for tungsten illumination (3200 K). The main drawback with this film is that it is only available in 30 m lengths and is, therefore, only really useful when you need a great deal of high quality work.

The most convenient light source, however, is electronic flash. This provides constant and readily available illumination and helps you to achieve consistent results. And if your copier has no iris diaphragm, you can vary the exposure simply by moving the flashgun, which must be on manual operation. Doubling the distance between gun and duplicator, for instance, reduces the effective exposure by 75 per cent. Calculations, though, are complex, and the best way to find the correct exposure is to make a series of test exposures with the flashgun 17, 25, 35, 50, 70, 100 and 141 cm from the copier. The distance that gives the correct exposure can be used for all similar slides.

The main advantage of using small flash units is that daylight film can be used and, unlike a tungsten light source, it does not cause heat problems. The need to have sufficient illumination to focus and set up is the main snag.

Bench top copiers

The third alternative procedure—a bench top copier—for producing duplicate transparencies is the most expensive. In many cases these copiers require a lens other than a normal camera lens for best results but, once the technical operations are mastered, they are able to provide the highest quality duplicates consistently and easily. They usually have the added advantage of using daylight film.

The facilities offered by bench top copiers vary. Some have built-in colour correction filters, while others merely have filter trays. Nearly all such copiers have a method of reducing contrast by giving an overall low-intensity fogging exposure across the entire frame.

As with the simpler systems described earlier, and no matter which individual bench-copier is chosen, tests have still to be made to determine the relationship between the lens, the light source, the film type and batch, the exposure necessary at differing degrees of enlargement and the amount of contrast control needed. All these tests have to be carried out with a 'standard' transparency before the unit can be used.

Once this transparency has been 'programmed', high quality duplicates of similar slides can be produced.

General copying principles

In practice, for facsimile reproduction of transparencies there are a number of factors which should always be borne in mind, no matter which procedure is being used.

Make sure that the originals are clean and dust free—scratches or drying marks will always appear far worse on the duplicate. The best way of cleaning a slide is to use an aerosol-type cleaner, which allows you to direct a jet of gas into the corners of the mount where dust tends to lurk.

Details that have been lost through overexposure in the original cannot be recovered. It is possible to make substantial improvements with off-colour or

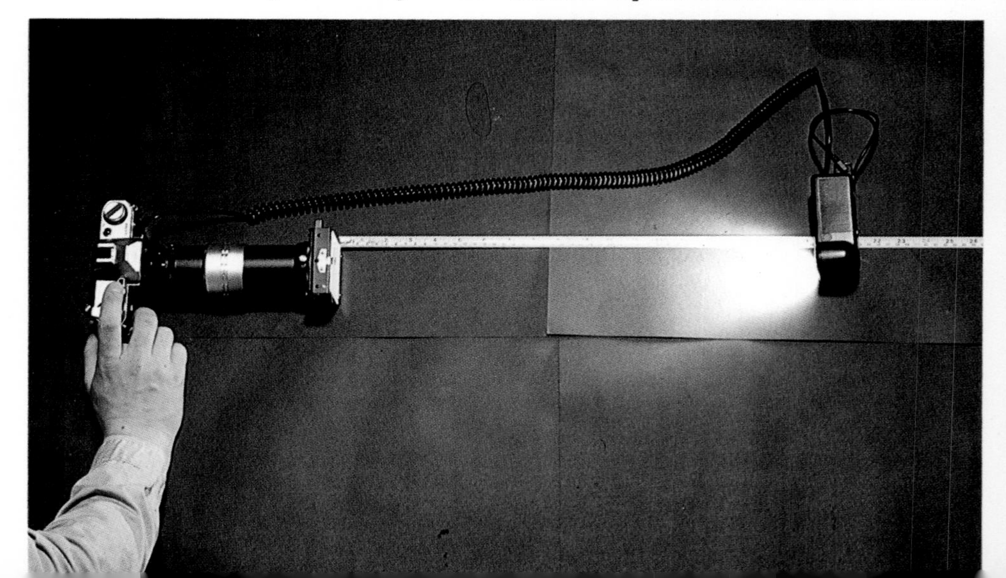

Exposure *For good results, you must shoot a test roll. Place a small flash gun at a range of distances from the copier and pick the best exposure*

140 cms

100 cms

70 cms

50 cms

35 cms

25 cms

17 cms

Test Roll *After processing, work out how far apart the flash and copier were for the best exposure, and use this separation whenever film of the same speed is in the camera. Here the best distance was found to be 100 cm*

underexposed transparencies, but not with slides that are too thin and pale.

Colour cannot be changed selectively, but colour casts can be removed or added. Always check the original visually with and without the correction filter to see whether the filter gives the correct colour balance.

Take extra trouble with slides which have soft pastel hues or a generally monochromatic appearance. They require care in order to achieve good quality duplicates, particularly in terms of contrast and colour control.

Contrast control

The big problem with slide copying is the inordinate gain in contrast in the duplicate. This occurs because, just as the brightness range in the subject far exceeded the exposure range of the film on which the original was made, so the brightness range in the slide far exceeds the exposure range of the film used for the duplicate. The result is that shadows in the duplicate become clogged and lacking in detail while the highlights tend to wash out altogether.

There are a number of solutions to this problem but one of the simplest is to make the copy on special duplicating film. This is very slow, but it has very fine grain characteristics and gives very low contrast results.

Duplicating films are, like Kodak's 5071, balanced for tungsten light; others, like Kodak's SE 371, are balanced for daylight. You should match the film to your copying light—the daylight film, of course, is suitable for copies made by flash. However, you should also match your duplicating film to your original film—both should be made by the same manufacturer. This is

New York train ***Shots with subtle but fairly high-contrast lighting tend to copy very badly—at very least pre-fogging is needed, and contrast-masking would be preferable. Without this kind of care, all the details in the shadows and the delicate golden sunlight would be lost in a duplicate.***

because each manufacturer biases film towards a certain colour and a mismatch of original and duplicating film types can give some fairly unpleasant colour casts.

If you cannot find a duplicating film to match, you may have to try alternative methods of reducing contrast in the copy slide.

The most widely used technique is to give the duplicate a brief fogging flash with white light before the main exposure. This fogging flash must be very weak—about two per cent of the main exposure—but it is enough to lighten the shadows a little, without significantly affecting the mid-tones and highlights.

Many bench-top slide copiers give the fogging flash automatically. The Bowens Illumitran, for instance, has a bolt-on contrast reducing unit that delivers the fogging flash in a precisely-controlled dose. Otherwise you can give the extra fogging exposure by making a double exposure. The first exposure is the brief fogging exposure; the second is the main exposure. By far the simplest way of controlling the fogging exposure is to place a 2.0 neutral density filter over the lens (or the flash) while you give an exposure equivalent to the main exposure.

An alternative way to reduce contrast is to slightly overexpose the duplicate and then underdevelop to compensate. This is quite effective, but not entirely predictable and is only really viable if you have your own processing facilities, so that you can make carefully calculated variations in processing.

Contrast control masks

The most effective way of controlling contrast is to make contrast control masks. Contrast control masks are very thin black and white negative copies of the original slide. They are made by exposing a length of black and white film in contact with the slide for a fraction of the time needed to give a full density negative (established by testing). This black and white mask is then held in contact with the original slide while the duplicate is made. The highlights in the negative have some density and so mask off the highlights in the slide, reducing its brightness range. The effect is, of course, progressive, and mid-tones are masked less, shadows not at all. This brings the brightness range of the slide within the exposure range of the duplicating film and so helps give a good range of tones in the copy.

Although this technique is very effective, and gives the best possible results, it is also very complex and long-winded—particularly as it is often necessary to make highlight masks as well to improve detail in the highlights. Contrast masks are really for those occasions when you want absolutely perfect copies. For most purposes, copies made on duplicating film or with pre-fogging are quite adequate. If you do want copies of a very high standard, it may be worth making the copies on large format film, such as 5 x 4 in sheet film.

Big wheel ***Set a bright red subject against a clear blue sky and use a polarizing filter to make it richer***

Slide combinations

Slide copying can be used for much more than simply producing exact duplicates of an original transparency. By combining pictures it is possible, even with fairly simple equipment, to create fantastic or graphic images. You can turn dull or unsuccessful shots into interesting pictures and produce effects which cannot be achieved any other way.

The advantage of working from transparencies is that it is relatively easy to imagine the final effect beforehand. There is no reason why you should only use ordinary colour slides; black and white and colour negatives, lith negatives and positives, coloured gels, tinted pictures and so on can all be combined. The possiblities are endless, and to get the most out of this type of work it is essential to experiment. The techniques in this article simply provide a few basic ideas to get you started.

Misty mountains *An ethereal effect has been created here by adding a separate cloud shot to the mountain picture*

Choosing the pictures

One of the first things you have to do is to decide which pictures you are going to combine. There is always some loss of quality when a picture is copied, so the shots you use should be technically good. Badly underexposed, high contrast or unsharp pictures should be avoided.

The best pictures are those which are fairly simple. Heavily detailed shots often make confused and messy combinations It is usually better to have the main subject, such as a face, surrounded by a plain tone or simple texture. This allows detail to show through from another slide.

Having chosen a range of shots, it is a good idea to plan the combinations on a lightbox. Number the pictures so that when you find a promising combination you can simply note the numbers down. This saves time when it comes to actually copying the pictures. To avoid damaging the shots through constant handling it is best to put them in transparent sleeves so that they can be viewed while remaining protected.

Straightforward slide copying is described on pages 80 to 84 and the basic procedure for combinations is similar. In all cases, you should shoot test films. Once you have established a standard set-up, the exposures will be fairly constant. However it is still a good idea to bracket in steps of half a stop over a range of two stops—start with slightly more exposure than for a straight copy.

For most of these techniques, you need surprisingly little in the way of equipment. Even simple, fixed focus copiers (see page 81-2) can give sophisticated results. But if you want to do this type of work regularly, a few additional items may be useful. A movable slide holder, for instance, helps give you complete control over the composition. A copier which allows you to magnify part of the picture is also an advantage. Without doubt the best type of copier is the bench top type. Many of them have built-in meters and exposure compensation scales which are invaluable when you are combining two or more very different transparencies.

But whatever equipment you use, there are two main approaches—one is to

physically place the originals together as a *sandwich* and then copy them as if they were one shot, and the other method is to use multiple exposures, shooting each picture in turn on to the same frame of film.

Making sandwiches

Using two transparencies sandwiched together is by far the simplest method, and can be very effective. The best types of pictures to use are those which are high key or slightly pale, because when they are placed together they combine to give a normal density. Normal or underexposed shots often become too dark when added together.

If possible, always sandwich the transparencies emulsion to emulsion. This avoids problems with focusing and depth of field when duplicating. For the same reason the pictures should be bound together in a slide mount. If necessary, glass mounts can be used to keep the transparencies flat and in contact with each other.

Black and white negatives sandwiched with colour transparencies work quite well. And if you want to use black and white positives, these are easily made by copying or contact printing the negatives on to continuous tone film.

Sandwiching colour or black and white

Combination variations *These pictures show a variety of effects made possible by combining shots. Subtle pictures can be created with multiple exposure (above left), though the separate elements need careful positioning. Sandwiching shots (above) is a simpler technique, though still very effective. Sandwiches often work best when the original shots are quite simple (below left), or unusual, as in the shot using negative images (right)*

transparencies of different subjects to give a surreal, montage-like effect is interesting. But you should also consider sandwiching almost identical shots. For example, two shots of the same view where just part of the subject has moved slightly between exposures. Strange effects can also be achieved by sandwiching identical shots slightly out of register, especially if one of the transparencies is quite pale—perhaps a slightly overexposed duplicate made from the original picture.

Sandwiches do not necessarily have to consist of two photographs. You can, for instance, sandwich one transparency with coloured gels, paper or other translucent materials. The grain in paper can be used to give a textured effect. Gels can bring alive an otherwise dull shot by introducing a strong or vibrant colour, or they can be used to create mood. For example, a blue gel used with a transparency which has slightly pale highlights gives a moonlight effect, especially if the copy is underexposed by half a stop.

Gels are also useful for colouring selected areas of the picture. If you do this, make sure that the gel is not in contact with the transparency so that the edge of the gel is out of focus and does not show up as a hard line. This technique is useful for adding tone or colour to the sky in a landscape in a similar way to using a graduated filter.

Unusual combinations

If you are interested in producing odd colour combinations try putting together pictures taken on different film stocks, such as infrared. This works particularly well if the two pictures are identical except for the film used. Pairs of shots like this are easy to produce by copying a normal original on to another film. Although this technique does not work with infrared film, it works very well with other materials.

One of the best techniques is to sandwich the original slide with a copy or slide film processed in negative colour film chemicals, giving a little extra exposure to prevent the result becoming overdense. Processing in negative chemicals gives slides in which the colours appear as complementaries, objects which are yellow in the original appear blue, for example. The tones are also reversed as in a negative. When you make the copy for processing in negative chemicals, put the original in the copier the wrong way round so that the two pictures can be sandwiched emulsion to emulsion.

This technique can be used to produce a strangely coloured bas relief effect by sandwiching the original slide and the negative copy slightly out of register. But it is also possible to produce bas reliefs with black and white materials. A negative sandwiched with a positive (produced by contact printing the negative on to film) gives an interesting three-dimensional effect. The negative should be quite thin to allow some tones to show. Coloured gels can be added to the sandwich and the whole copied on to colour slide film. The positive can also be toned the same or different colours with a wide range of special darkroom techniques and systems.

One problem which often crops up when copying is high contrast, particularly when you are making a copy of a copy. But contrast is relatively easy to reduce by using masks. Contact printing the original on to Kodak Pan Masking Film 4570 gives a negative which, when sandwiched with the original, reduces the brightness of the highlights (see page 84).

These low contrast masks can also be coloured using the Colorvir process. Alternatively, the mask can be copied on to colour transparency film using a coloured gel and the copy sandwiched with the original.

Going to the other extreme, high contrast masks, produced by contact printing the original on to line or lith film, can give very dramatic results. By varying the exposure when making the masks you can control which parts of the picture go dark. For example, you can produce jet black clouds floating in a red sunset.

Multiple exposure duplication

In spite of the versatility of sandwiching, there are some effects which can only be achieved by using multiple exposures, or which can be done better in this way. If, for example, you want to add a large moon to a landscape shot, double exposure is by far the best technique. Simply sandwiching the two shots would give a moon where the highlights are degraded by the tone in the sky. Double exposure causes the highlights to burn out because you are adding light rather than subtracting it. So with this method the highlights come out bright and clear.

The other main advantage with multiple exposure is that it allows masks to be used. If you want to use just part of a picture the rest can be masked off with thin black card. For best results the card should not be in contact with the transparency but held slightly above it to give a soft edge. Cutting and using masks is not easy, but with practice quite spectacular combinations are possible.

The principal difficulty with multiple exposure, particularly when you are using masks, is in getting the pictures properly aligned. It is possible to use sketches of the various elements of the picture as seen in the viewfinder as a rough guide, but this can never be completely accurate. A feature which is very useful for this technique is a focusing screen with a grid marked on it. This type of screen is available as an accessory for most cameras which have interchangeable screens. The grid makes it much easier to sketch the view through the finder. A better method is to use a camera with a detachable viewfinder, such as the Pentax LX. With the finder removed, the position of the first transparency can be marked directly on to the focusing screen with a wax pencil. Subsequent transparencies are then aligned with this sketch.

Another problem you may encounter is the lack of a double exposure facility on your camera. All cameras can be made to give multiple exposures in some way but there is often some inaccuracy in registration. If you intend doing a great deal of combination work, it is worth considering buying a camera with a built-in multiple exposure facility. The alternative is to work in a darkened room, with the camera shutter set on 'B', firing the flash manually for each picture. However, this method does not allow you to check the positions of the shots at all and so is not recommended when accurate alignment is needed.

Colour posterization

With the multiple exposure technique it is also possible to make colour posterization directly in the camera. The basic procedure for posterization is to make three copies of the original, one normally exposed, one overexposed and the other under exposed—called 'tone separations'. These separations are made on lith film from an original—either black and white or colour—and these are rephotographed in contact with coloured filters.

The separations can be negatives, positives or a combination of both. Registration is the major problem if complete accuracy is wanted. One solution is to tape the separations to the copier in such a way that they can be flipped in front of the lens in turn. You

Handling slides *For maximum protection it is best to keep the pictures in transparent sleeves when sorting them*

Projected combinations *Images projected on to a screen can be photographed with a camera placed behind the projectors*

Moon shot *Adding the moon is best done using multiple exposure, which ensures that the highlights remain bright.*
Beach relief *This bas relief effect was created by combining a toned black and white mask with the original.*
Scapegoat *Combining pictures in a duper is the ideal way of producing surreal or fantastic images*

should make tests and experiment to find the best colour combinations and exposures. Exposures in particular are often difficult to judge. Generally you should follow the procedure for normal multiple exposures, splitting the exposure time. But you should always bracket and try giving each picture being copied a different level of exposure.

When adding the moon to the landscape, for instance, you may find that the standard multiple exposure procedure gives a correctly exposed landscape but a moon which is too bright. To compensate for this you have to keep the landscape exposure the same while reducing the exposure for the moon. This is relatively easy if you are using a sophisticated bench-top copier. But with simpler equipment it requires some experimentation.

Projected combinations

One way of producing combinations without using a slide copier is to project the pictures on to a screen and rephotograph them. Two or more projectors are lined up so that the images overlap. Ideally the projectors should have identical light sources so that there is no difference in illumination between the various pictures. The best equipment is that used for A–V shows. In particular, a fade–dissolve facility allows you to control the image very precisely.

The camera should be mounted on a tripod, since the exposures are likely to be too long for hand-held shots. A medium telephoto lens is the most useful for this work as it allows you to shoot from behind the projection equipment and so avoids the problem of the camera getting in the way of the projector. Built-in exposure meters are adequate for determining the correct exposure, but it is better to use a hand-held meter, measuring using the incident method (see 13). It is also advisable to bracket exposures by half stops to allow for uneven tone distribution in the image. Do not use too slow a shutter speed or the film will suffer from reciprocity failure giving underexposure and a colour cast. You should also remember to use artificial light film.

Slides can be projected on to white walls, draped fabric, white painted objects, the human figure, masks and so on. Some specialist photographic shops sell a range of materials designed for diffusing lights which can make unusual and interesting projection screens. Any part of a slide which is not wanted in the final image can be masked out using black card. The card is held in front of and quite near to the projector lens. In this way the edges of the card remain out of focus.

Whichever method you choose for combining pictures it is important to spend some time on it. Only by experimenting can you find the technique which best suits the type of image you are after. With just a few basic pictures you can produce a wide range of images and once you have gained some experience in this type of work you can also start to shoot various pictures with combinations in mind.

Make your own lightbox

A lightbox is an accessory which few photographers would put near the top of a list of essential items. But its usefulness and versatility make it the sort of unit which, once you have one, rapidly becomes indispensable, and after a while you wonder how you ever managed without it.

As well as its obvious use for sorting slides, a lightbox can be used for examining negatives, cutting and tracing film, spotting out defects on negatives, providing illumination for copying transparent objects, and even for giving a diffuse source of light for black and white studio work.

Probably the main reason that more amateurs do not own lightboxes is that they are comparatively expensive—particularly if they are of a larger size rather than being small slide sorters. But if you make your own, you can own one for quite a small outlay. The work involved can be handled by anyone with a small range of tools and an elementary knowledge of wiring.

Although this article describes a specific unit, the basic instructions can easily be adapted to suit your own requirements. You could, for example, build it into a working surface in the darkroom, or elsewhere.

Lightbox application

Before you start to make a lightbox you should consider the conditions under which it will be used, as these determine the design and type of the important lighting elements it will contain. Tube length and wattage influence the light output of the lightbox, so before you choose the lighting tubes decide where your lightbox will be used. A lightbox used in a brightly lit office has much lower apparent brightness, or *luminosity,* than if it was used in somewhere like a darkroom, even though its actual, measurable brightness, or *luminance,* remains the same. In fact, in poor lighting, the glare of a bright lightbox can cause acute discomfort, especially if you have to switch continuously between the two extremes for viewing and working.

For a low output lightbox, simply use the shortest length of tube you can. For high output, fit as many tubes into the available lightbox enclosure as possible. Alternatively make a high output box with switches that allow some tubes to be switched off—then you can use the lightbox in dark and bright conditions.

Home-made lightbox *Although the cost of the lighting components can be high, making your own lightbox can save you a great deal of money. The design for this box is shown opposite*

Tube types

Many types of tube can be used in a lightbox. All will provide the necessary light to illuminate the slide but the 'warm' ones, in particular, may prove quite unsuitable for accurate colour assessment. If this is an essential requirement—where it is vital to match colours from a photographic, rather than visual, point of view—then special tubes such as Graphica 47 must be used. These are about five times the cost of the 'ordinary' tubes listed, so for general purpose work choose bulbs from the top half of the table (over).

The efficacy of a tube is its lumens/watts rating and indicates the relative brightness when tubes are compared. A low efficacy tube combined with a thick diffuser may mean that more tubes than normal may be needed for a certain level of luminance. High efficacy tubes should be chosen when the fewest possible tubes are required for a lightbox with high luminance.

Although most tubes are straight, circular (warm white) and U-shaped tubes (white, warm white and plus white) can be used instead. One manufacturer even provides a 'concertina' form (daylight) with a power and light output to match a straight 2400 mm tube (see illustration). These shaped tubes enable you to cram a lot of tube power into a fairly constricted space.

The lightbox shown here was designed for four 600 mm tubes, but could accommodate as many as six—or as little as two—with only slight modification.

Controls and wiring

Fluorescent tubes need special control gear to provide high enough voltage to initiate the discharge which causes the tube to light. Various methods are employed but one of the simplest consists of a simple choke or capacitor ballast (or a combination of both) operated in series with the tube. A starter switch is connected across the lamp to initiate the striking sequence, a standard method now used for most domestic applications. A typical circuit is shown, along with a circuit diagram for four controls as used in the lightbox design shown here. It is based on the use of ready assembled control units which need only be connected to a switched and fused mains supply for use.

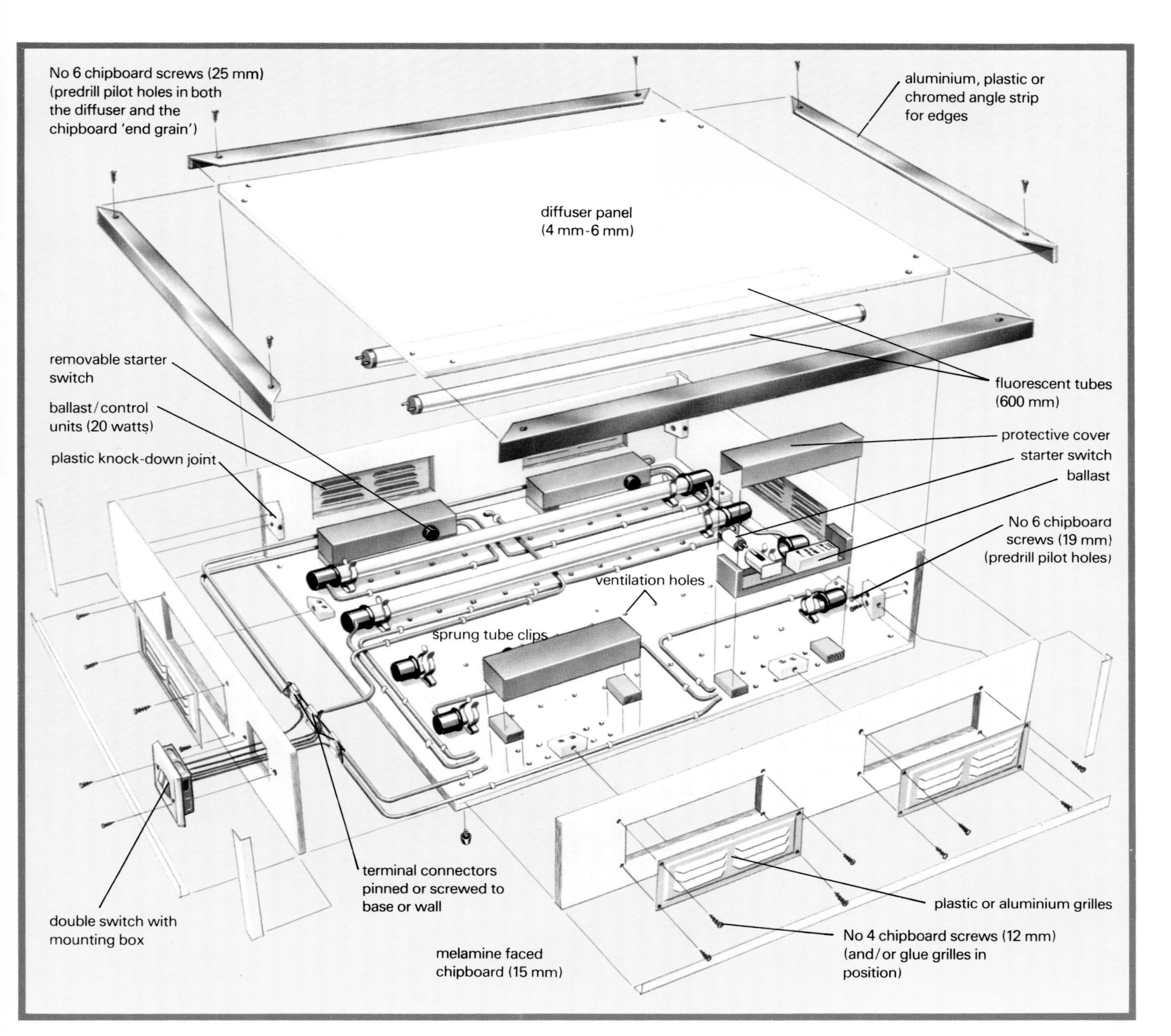

Replacement tubes

Tubes have a useful working life of around 7500 hours—or longer if you can tolerate working with light output fall off—so many years may pass before a replacement becomes necessary. Tubes which need replacing more frequently include those used for colour balancing and assessment. All tubes should be replaced if blackening of the tube phosphor occurs at each end—but by this stage light output is likely to have reached an unacceptably low level.

If you are planning to make a fairly lightweight, portable lightbox, there is a much greater risk of tube failure caused by physical damage. No tube is likely to withstand constant jarring without suffering—and those fixed rigidly to the structure of the lightbox may well smash if the lightbox itself is badly knocked or dropped. Loosely fitted tubes may smash against the interior of the box.

Unless the tube comes with its own batten fitting, use proper tube clips to keep it firmly in position. Plastic types have enough 'give' to absorb all but the hardest knocks a lightbox may receive.

Solidly constructed desk lightboxes need not be provided with an access panel for tube or starter replacement—this occasional job can be done by removing the diffuser panel, for instance. But do allow at least some means of access otherwise you may have to destroy at least part of your construction if a fault occurs.

Incorporate a special access panel if you are designing a lightweight, portable lightbox. For example, use external screw fixings for the base (or one of the sides) rather than nails, glue or internal fixings.

When thinking about tube life, remember that frequent switching, combined with short running periods, can seriously accelerate tube failure—and these are precisely the sort of conditions to which a lightbox is subjected. A tube's rated life is usually based on a continuous running time for each start of three hours. By cutting this to one hour's continuous use each start—probably far longer than required for the occasional use of an amateur lightbox—the rated life is cut by half.

The diffuser panel

White opalized acrylic sheet is the best material to use for the diffuser panel but PVC or polystyrene sheet with the same transmission characteristics may prove suitable. However, these are rather brittle by comparison.

Acrylic sheet 4 to 6 mm thick provides the best compromise between transmittance and dimensional strength needed for a panel supported by its edges only. Opal acrylic sheet may be available in various diffusion strengths. Perspex '050' grade, with 45 per cent transmittance is preferable to the '030' grade (78 per cent transmittance) as its diffusion characteristics are very much better—but more tubes may be needed to compensate for the much higher light loss.

Suppliers will cut sheet precisely to size. You can get the edges polished smooth at the same time, for a small additional fee—and this may considerably enhance the appearance of your completed lightbox where the edges remain visible.

The panel can be fixed in several ways to the top of the lightbox. The material is easily worked using normal woodwork tools and can be drilled to accept screws, perhaps the simplest method of fixing. Use a countersink bit so that the screw head lies flush or beneath the surface of the diffuser.

Another method is to use plastic or metal angle strip to anchor the sheet in position by its edges. This strip could also be used to finish off any other method of fixing—chrome strips would give a very professional finish.

Yet another method is to use small mirror clips (as also used for pinning glass to a picture, or glass to a table).

Finally—and if your woodworking skills are up to is—actually rebate the sheet edges in the sides of the lightbox. No additional panel support should be necessary if the panel fits the grooved recesses tightly all round.

Acrylic sheet is very easily scratched and so you should avoid cutting directly on a diffuser panel made of this. But one of the attractions of a lightbox is that you can do all your viewing and 'bagging up' operations and negative cutting more or less simultaneously, using the lightbox rather like a worktop.

Some protection can be provided during actual cutting operations by using a thick sheet of plate or float glass placed on the plastic diffuser.

But if you plan to use your lightbox mostly for trimming and cutting—rather than simply for viewing—it may be better to use white opalized plate of float glass for the diffuser panel. Glass is not without its disadvantages, however—it is extremely expensive in opalized form, is heavy and it must be of the correct thickness for any given area, remembering it receives support only at the edges. It is also very easily cracked and therefore quite unsuitable for a portable unit.

Glass which is 4 mm or 6 mm thick should be suitable for a small size lightbox using 20 watt or 30 watt tubes. This can be fixed in position with angle strip or mirror clips, or by screws if you can have the glass drilled to accept these. As a precaution, particularly if the edge is left exposed after fixing, ask the glazier to polish the edges smooth.

Ventilation

Tubes operate best in ambient temperatures of around 25°C. But the enclosed space of a lightbox can act like an oven to raise the operating, or *tube-wall* temperature to levels way in excess of the normal ideal, 40°C. Air temperature within the lightbox at 50°C, for instance, results in a tube wall temperature of about 70°C. This results in a light output drop to about 70 per cent.

While this reduction of light output is merely inconvenient, the heat generated by the tube and its control gear must be checked by adequate ventilation of the lightbox interior. Otherwise you risk damaging the lightbox diffuser panel or overheating material placed on the lightbox for viewing. More serious are the risks of high levels of transmitted heat which could cause personal injury on contact, as well as constituting a very real fire risk.

Ballasts employed in the control gear can attain surface temperatures of 100°C even under normal conditions—and sig-

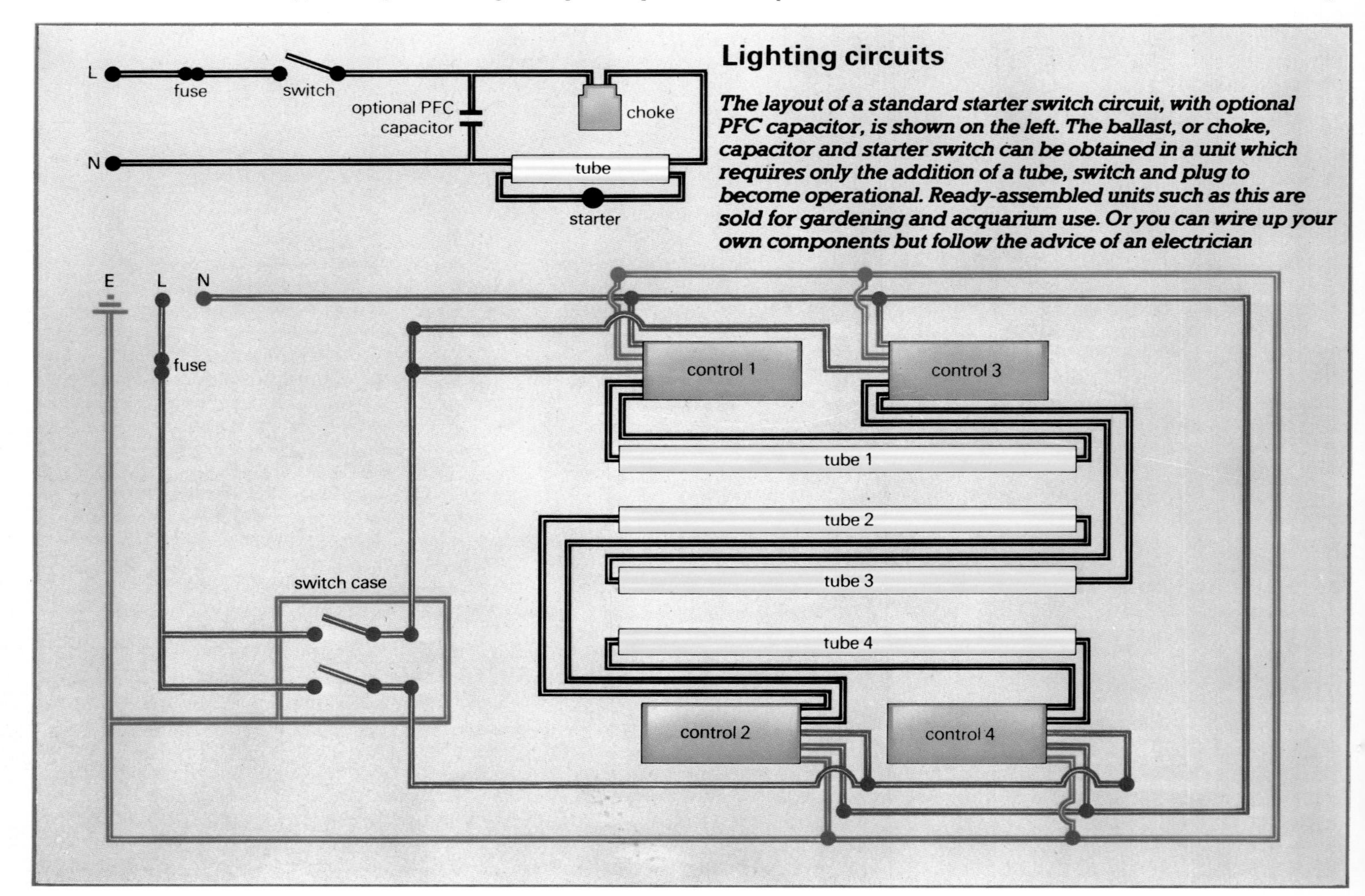

Lighting circuits

The layout of a standard starter switch circuit, with optional PFC capacitor, is shown on the left. The ballast, or choke, capacitor and starter switch can be obtained in a unit which requires only the addition of a tube, switch and plug to become operational. Ready-assembled units such as this are sold for gardening and acquarium use. Or you can wire up your own components but follow the advice of an electrician

Retouching *A useful application of a lightbox is to provide good back-lighting for retouching—a frequent and often necessary chore if you use lith film*
Cutting *If you use your lightbox for cutting film in strips, or to size, place a sheet of glass on top first to prevent scratches. Have the edges ground smooth. Use thick plate or float glass, of the strengthened type if possible.*
Tube type *You may choose to use shaped tubes (far right) in your design. Miniature tubes are available also*

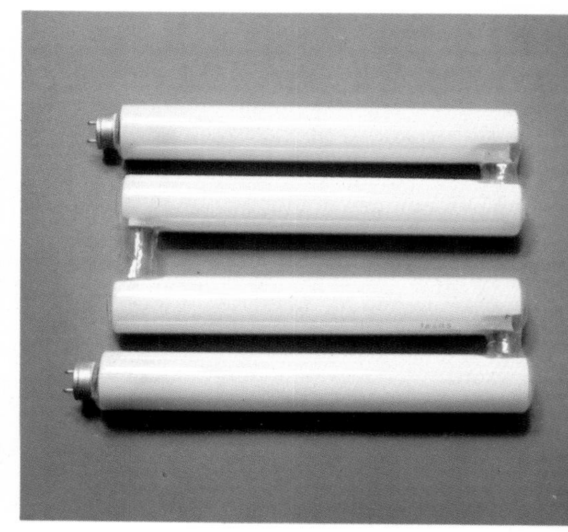

nificantly more in a lightbox enclosure. It is this component of a fluorescent light fitting which needs particular attention when you are planning your lightbox design. If it forms part of a complete control unit, this should be treated like an independent ballast and located well away from the diffuser but near to ventilated grilles or holes provided for cooling.

A simple system of grilles or holes along each side of the lightbox can prove entirely adequate, though grilles are neater. The main problem with these simple systems is that they must extend to all sides of the lightbox to be effective—and this results in a substantial amount of light leakage which may prove unacceptable. However, a slightly more involved lightbox construction enables you to use a baffle system to cut down this annoying spillage.

All-in-one control units can safely be located outside the lightbox enclosure, ideally in a well beneath. This could be open to the air, or provided with generously sized ventilation holes or grilles. Only minimal ventilation need then be provided for the tubes.

Tube characteristics

Tube colour	Colour temperature	Colour appearance	Colour rendering	Efficacy (l/w)	Usual application
Artificial daylight	6500K	cool	excellent	30	low efficiency but best colour rendering
Northlight/ Colour matching	6500K	cool	excellent	42	accurate matching of colours
Daylight (cool white)	4300K	cool	fair	67	general purpose: to blend with daylight
Kolor-rite	4000K	neutral	excellent	46	best colour rendering for general lighting
Natural	4000K	neutral	good	52	general lighting applications
Plus white	3600K	neutral	good	67	general lighting with good rendering
White	3400K	neutral	fair	70	general lighting at maximum efficiency
Warm white	3000K	warm	fair	69	general lighting at high efficiency
Home-lite (USA)	2600K	warm	good	62	for giving interiors a 'warm' appearance

Lightbox construction

Melamine faced chipboard or other plastic coated board is probably the best of all the wood-based materials that could conceivably be used for constructing the actual lightbox. Its one drawback is that it is thick and therefore heavy. But otherwise it is easily worked and requires no painting. You can use white melamine faced board for the lightbox interior, and patterned board for the exterior if the same board does not serve both functions.

Manmade board of this type is usually sold for shelving or for simple furniture construction, and is usually available in a set range of lengths and widths. Shelving widths would be suitable for making the lightbox walls, but a much wider piece would be needed for the base—and it is this that should influence the design of your lightbox. Shelving up to 60 cm wide is perfectly suitable for a lightbox similar to the design shown here.

The easiest method of joining the board is to use knock-down plastic block joints located at the ends of each join. The various pieces can be sawn to make butt joints as shown in the various box designs, then drilled, to provide ventilation holes prior to assembly.

However, you may prefer to use a system of pin/dowel joints in conjunction with corner and edge supports cut from suitable pieces of planed softwood. This gives a much stronger box construction.

Plywood is another very useful material for lightbox construction, but must be properly painted afterwards. Use WBP ('water and boil proof') or exterior grade ply as these are less likely to suffer from the heat build up within the lightbox.

Paints used for interior finish should be brilliant white, glossy or matt, but—above all—capable of withstanding high temperatures. Your local supplier should be able to help you choose something suitable. Radiator paints and paints specified as being suitable for painting hot pipes can be used.

Chapter 8

FILTER CONTROL
Balancing colour

Colour correction aids *vary greatly in price and complexity but they are indispensable under certain conditions*

Correcting for the colour temperature of lighting can be a headache for any photographer using slide film. But while it is not difficult to assess the approximate colour of the light source and take corresponding steps to correct for colour casts and balance with filters, accurate colour balance requires great care.

Further, lighting conditions, particularly outdoors, can change so rapidly that while deciding which correction filter to use, you miss the shot. However, all this can be simplified and considerably speeded up if you use a colour temperature meter to take the guesswork out of assessment and have an appropriate range of filter types to draw upon, following the meter's recommendations.

Unfortunately, colour temperature meters are fairly expensive—on average about the same as a medium priced SLR —and even many professionals do without one. However the justification for buying such a meter largely depends on the kind of work you do. For example, where your shots have to be spot-on first time and the lighting conditions are likely to be very variable or unpredictable, a colour meter can soon pay for itself in terms of time and film saved.

Conversion or compensation?

There are two ranges of filter types which can be used to correct for colour temperature conditions which do not match the film you are using—*colour conversion* (light balancing) and *colour compensating* filters. The difference between the two is that conversion filters, such as the 80A or 81B, effectively convert one light source into another by an overall change, while compensating filters, such as a 20M or 40G allow you to make small changes to each colour component of the light. They are much more versatile than conversion filters, but to give a range wide enough to cope with most situations, you need many more filters.

Every user of slide film should have a basic set of conversion filters. Unquestionably the most useful is the 81B, which is also known as a 'cloudy day filter'. Some photographers, however, use the milder version of this, the 81A, permanently on their lenses in place of the skylight or UV filter, to protect the front element of the lens. An 81A also helps to reduce the blue cast on flesh tones when using electronic flash.

Less useful for general work is the 82 series, though an 82B may be handy for occasions when the sun has a distinct reddish cast which you wish to avoid. An 80B is worth having, since it allows you to use daylight film in tungsten lighting, while an 85B does the reverse—it enables you to use tungsten balanced film (Type B) in daylight.

So a useful basic outfit would include an 80B, an 81B, an 82B and an 85B. In all cases the B filter of the series has a more noticeable effect than the A filter, so if you only want one filter it is probably better to aim for one that has a noticeable effect, to give you a greater range. Remember that the 81 and 82 series have equal but opposite effects, so the only result of combining filters from both series will be to cut down the light—just like a neutral-density filter.

Mireds and filters

Conversion filters can be given values on what is called the *mired* scale. The word mired—pronounced *my-red*—is short for *micro reciprocal degrees*. Any colour temperature has a mired value, found by dividing that temperature into one million.

The advantage of this is that a colour conversion filter can be given a constant mired value—for example, an 81B has a mired value of +27. This can be used to predict the effect it will have on a light source of any colour temperature: it makes it redder by 27 mireds. Such a scale is useful because if there is very little blue in the light, an 81B will have a comparatively small influence on the blue proportion of the light—that is, it raises or lowers colour temperature less than when there is a great deal of blue around. For this reason, it is usual to convert both filters and colour temperatures to the mired scale. On colour temperature meters, this is in the form of *decamireds* (units of ten mireds)—the +27 of an 81B is rounded off to +30, and called 3R. A similar strength bluish filter, with a negative mired value, would have a value of 3B.

Colour compensation

In the case of colour compensating (CC) filters, a basic kit is less easy to decide on. There are six strengths available in each of the primary and complementary colours, which gives a total range of 36 filters.

Filters ***Light balancing filters are available in shades of either blue or yellow, but CC filters are more varied***

They can be used in combination, except that it is pointless to combine a primary with its complementary—that is, red with cyan, green with magenta and blue with yellow.

CC filters are used to filter out individual colours entering the lens, unlike the conversion or light balancing filters, which are used to adjust only the overall colour of the light. They are equivalent to the filters used in the darkroom in colour printing.

In practice, only green and magenta filters are usually needed if you already have a set of 80, 81, 82 and 85 conversion filters. They are needed to correct for the colour of such artificial light sources as fluorescent light and some street lights. It is also possible to buy conversion filters, such as the FL/D, which approximately convert fluorescent light to daylight. But even these filters are not the complete answer—ideally, a separate compensation filter pack is needed for each type of fluorescent light. Although Kodak advise on the choice of filters for any given type of fluorescent tube, there may still be casts caused by such factors as the age or make of the tube.

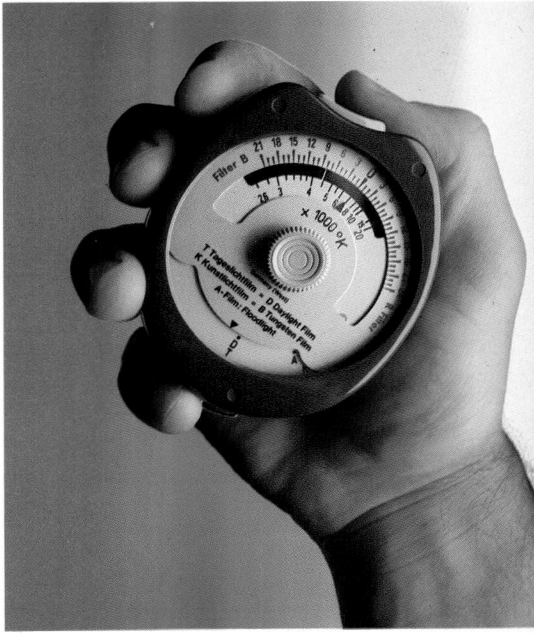

The Sixticolor meter *records colour temperatures through a metering cell on the back of the instrument*

Filter values and colour temperatures *are read off the scale and the filter number is obtained from a table*

The only sure way to correct for such lighting is to take a trial series using the recommended filter pack, then make further correction if necessary.

Another use for colour compensating filters is to correct for known deficiencies of the film, such as colour casts resulting from the age of the film or from reciprocity failure effects. If you discover that a particular batch of film has, say, a cyan cast you can correct for this using a red filter—a CC 10R may be enough.

Colour compensating filters are usually only available as gelatin, which is comparatively cheap, but they must be

A Profisix lightmeter *can, with a simple attachment, be converted into a colour temperature meter*

The Profi-color *attachment clips on to the Profisix, and a colour calculator is placed over the scale*

used in special square technical filter holders. Filters used for colour printing purposes may be suitable as long as their optical quality allows them to be used below the lens—which many cannot. A full set will enable you to correct for practically any colour imbalance that may be present—but to choose the filters which match the light source, you must rely on experience, manufacturers' guidelines, or a colour temperature meter.

Colour temperature meters

Most colour temperature meters work simply by metering red and blue light separately and then comparing their intensity. The simplest, most popular and least expensive meter on the market, the German Gossen Sixticolor, illustrates the principle well.

The Sixticolor has two selenium cells, needing no battery. One cell is covered by a blue-green filter and the other by a red-orange filter. The outputs from both cells are fed to a meter in opposition to each other. So when the proportions of red and blue light are equal, the meter is exactly balanced and gives a zero reading. But if there is a greater proportion of one or the other the needle will be deflected, giving an indication on a scale of decamireds which can then be converted into filter values. It also has a straightforward colour temperature scale.

The Sixticolor measures colour temperature from 2600K to 20,000K—a range which includes at the red end the light from a 40W domestic bulb, and at the other end the bluest outdoor daylight, in which the subject is lit only by a blue sky with the sun behind a cloud.

When using the meter, there is no need to adjust for light intensity—it reads in all normal lighting conditions. First you set the film type, rather than speed—daylight, photoflood or tungsten. Then you point the meter directly at the light source, and note the meter reading in mireds—it will give a filter value of up to 21B units (indicating that a bluish filter is needed) or 24R units (a reddish filter). A table supplied with the meter gives the appropriate conversion filter, or pack of CC filters, for each reading. There are differences between the reference numbers used by Kodak, Agfa and some filter makers, so the tables are essential.

It is also possible to convert the Gossen Profisix light meter to read colour temperatures. The Profi-color attachment includes a meter cell and dial which clips over the normal light metering scales.

Filter equivalents

Different manufacturers use different names for colour correction fiilters. Here are some approximate equivalents (Agfa filters are not exactly the same strength as others).

Decamired	Wratten	Agfa
R1.5	1A	CTO 1B
R3	81B	CTO 2B
R9	85C	CTO 8B
R12	85	CTO 12B
B3	82B	CTB 2
B12	80B	CTB 12

Basic conversion filters for different film types

Lighting	Film	Filter
daylight	daylight	none
	type A	85C
	type B	85
photofloods or QI	daylight	80C
	type A	none
	type B	81A
domestic tungsten or floods	daylight	80B
	type A	82A
	type B	none
warm white fluorescent	daylight	82B+20M
	type A	85C+20M
	type B	81EF+ 81C+20M

Minolta Color Meter II

A much more elaborate and expensive meter, the Minolta Color Meter II works on the same basic principle as the Gossen Sixticolor, but instead has three cells, covering red, green and blue parts of the spectrum, and uses microelectronics to compare their outputs and give a reading. It has a switch to program daylight (5500K) photoflood (3400K) or tungsten film (3200K), but can also handle any other setting. Nevertheless, some films, usually balanced at 5350K might actually be balanced at 5350K. So if you wish to take full advantage of the meter, you must test the film batch to establish its true bias, using the meter and a series of filter combinations on a test film.

Readings can be taken in kelvins, mireds (called light balancing or LB values) and CC filter values in decamireds. A scale on the back of the meter converts the mired values into Wratten filter descriptions, and CC decamired values into magenta or green filter numbers.

To use the meter, a button is pressed to select the type of film being used. Then a large metering button on the side is pressed for a few seconds to record and stabilize the reading—the liquid crystal display stays blank until the reading is computed and stored in the memory. You can then press the required function key for light balancing filter, CC filter or kelvin reading repeatedly, and the appropriate value will be displayed from the meter's memory.

For example, a reading taken in a tungsten lit office with daylight (5500K) film was 3270K, –2 units CC, –123 units LB. The scales on the back indicated an 80B plus an 82 blue light balancing filter, and a 05G green CC filter. Factors on the scales showed an exposure increase of $2\frac{1}{3}$ stops necessary with this filter pack.

In a room lit by fluorescent tubes with a magnolia painted ceiling, the reading was 4700K, +9CC, –31LB. This resulted in a filter pack of 82B plus 20M for daylight film, with one stop exposure increase. Switching to Type B film, the meter displayed +99 LB, +9 CC, which converted to 85C plus 81A and 20M: exposure increase was one stop. A colour temperature meter's readings are, however, likely to be inaccurate in any form of lighting which consists of a discrete line output and the readings may be untrustworthy.

Using the Minolta Color Meter II *Select the type of film being used and press the metering button on the right hand side of the meter long enough for the reading to be recorded and stored in the electronic memory. The LB key is pressed to display light balancing filter values; the CC key for colour correcting filters and the K key for colour temperatures. Filter numbers are tabulated on the back of the meter*

A reading taken in bright, overcast daylight gave +15 LB and –2 CC at 6000K. The recommended filters were 81A plus a 05G CC. The 81A is the usual filter to 'warm up' an overcast day, but the 05G is unexpected. It was needed because red-brick buildings surrounding the subject reflected a high proportion of red light.

The Minolta Color Meter II is the only popularly available meter of this type and will give readings for almost any film stock and light condition.

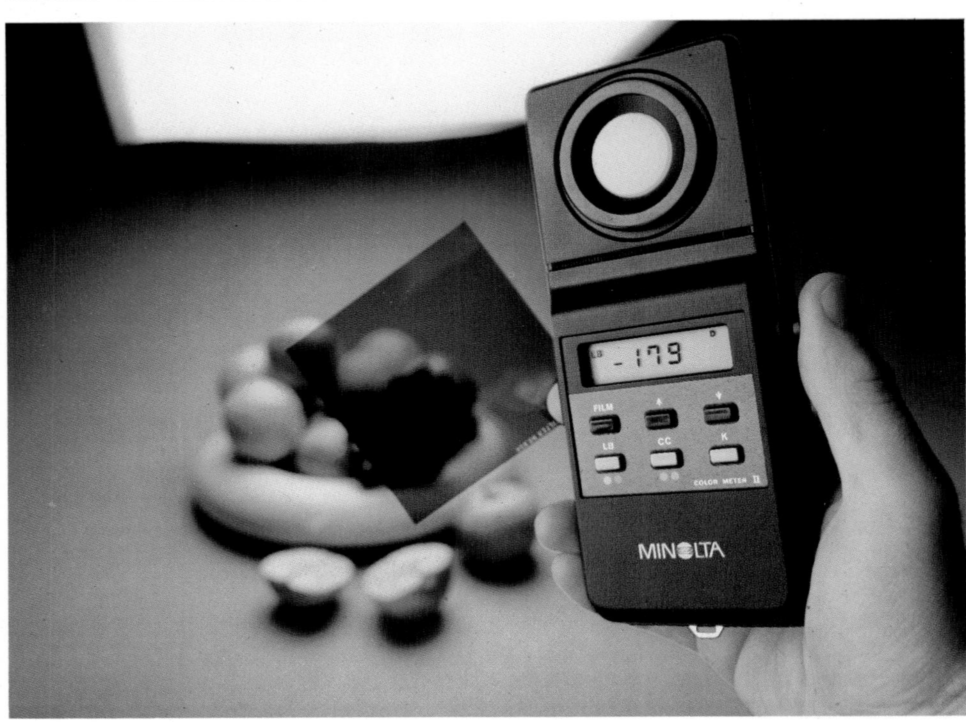

Controls *for selecting film type and preset or variable colour temperatures, are a feature of most meters*

Example reading *The Minolta Color Meter II here gives a light balancing filter reading of –179 for daylight film in tungsten light, and indicates the use of a Wratten 80A filter*

Filter guide

Many problems in photography can be overcome by the use of suitable coloured filters. And even simple filters can be used creatively to turn an ordinary shot into something worthwhile. As well as special effects filters, there are the straightforward gelatin filters, which are less often mentioned in catalogues. It is useful to know what types there are.

These pages provide a list of most of the filters available in gelatin form, which is the most versatile and wide ranging type. The numbers in the main list refer to the Kodak Wratten number, though the same numbers are used by most other manufacturers too. The filters in each section are listed in order of their density. The additional tables suggest ways of using some of these filters to correct for artificial lighting, and the final one shows exposure increases for a range of colour compensating filters, which are used to 'fine tune' colour temperature.

Pink

1A Pale pink These filters, often called *skylight* filters, are used to absorb excess UV radiation. For general photography they are of comparatively little use. However, they do have some effect in reducing the blueness caused by haze at high altitudes. They are also occasionally useful when there is a great deal of UV, such as a snow covered landscape under a blue sky, though an 81A is often better. The glass in modern lens elements usually filters out a sufficient amount of UV, though some photographers use glass versions of this filter as protection for their lenses, in place of the more usual UV types.

Yellows

Yellow filters also absorb ultraviolet radiation. They are sometimes used to filter for haze, particularly in black and white work, and are popular for aerial photography. They are also used to darken blue skies, and increase contrast with black and white film. The darker yellow filters are used with colour infrared (false colour) film to prevent the result being too blue.

2A Pale yellow Absorbs UV below 405 nm. Used to reduce haze at high altitudes
2B Pale yellow Absorbs UV below 390 nm. Better than 2A at reducing haze
2E Pale yellow Absorbs UV below 415 nm. Like the 2B but has more effect on UV
3 Light yellow Often used in aerial photography to correct for excess blue
8 Yellow Gives correct rendition of sky and foliage on black and white film
9 Deep yellow Similar to No. 8, but gives a stronger, more dramatic effect
11 Yellow–green Gives correct rendering in tungsten light on monochrome film
12 Deep yellow Used for haze penetration in aerial photography and for monochrome infrared materials
15 Deep yellow This produces even more dramatic effects than No. 8 or No. 9. It is used for black and white copying of documents on yellowed paper. It is also used for infrared and fluorescence photography

Oranges and reds

These filters are designed to absorb ultraviolet and blue, and also varying amounts of green. With black and white film they are used to increase contrast—for example, to darken blue skies, bring out the grain in wood, or pick out the detail in brick. Red filters are also used for technical work, such as colour separation, colour printing and two-colour photography. The last is a method of producing colour pictures by breaking down the image into two colour components.

16 Yellow–orange filters are mostly used for emphasizing detail in wood and brick, and also widely used for darkening blue skies, in both cases using black and white materials
21 Orange is the most popular orange filter, used to give greater contrast on black and white film
22 Deep orange Commonly used in photomicrography with blue preparations, this filter has greater green absorption than the other orange types
23A Light red Used in colour separation work and also for increased contrast with black and white film
24 Red is used mostly for two-colour photography in conjunction with a 57 (green) filter
25 Red One of the most useful red filters, the 25 reduces haze in black and white aerial shots and filters out excess blue light for monochrome infrared work. It is also used for colour separation and tricolour printing
29 Deep red Principally used for colour separation and tricolour printing

Magentas and violets

These filters principally absorb green, and are mostly used for technical applications, such as reproduction processes and photomicrography. Other magenta filters (CC filters) are used to correct for fluorescent light.

30 Light magenta Used in photomicrography to give increased contrast particularly with green subjects
32 Magenta Used to subtract green
33 Magenta absorbs green strongly and is used in colour reproduction processes to produce masks
34 Deep violet Contrast filter
35 Purple The main use for this filter is to provide contrast in photomicrography. It provides total green absorption and also absorbs some blue and red

Greens

These are mostly used for black and white photography as contrast filters (to lighten foliage for example) and in technical processes such as colour reproduction and colour printing.

54 Deep green This contrast filter absorbs nearly all red and blue light, and a little green light
57 Green Used for two-colour photography with a red (24) filter
58 Green Used as a contrast filter in photomicrography and also for colour separation and tricolour printing
61 Deep green Used for colour separation and tricolour printing work with red (29) and blue (47) filters

Blues and blue–greens

These filters are designed mainly for colour separation work, tricolour printing, contrast effects in photomicrography, and to heighten contrast in black and white work. Blue conversion and light balancing filters are dealt with in a separate section. On black and white film blue filters darken reds. By emphasizing blue tones they can be used to exaggerate mist or fog.

38 Light blue is useful in tungsten lighting with black and white film to prevent red tones from reproducing too light
38A Blue absorbs a large amount of red light, plus a certain amount of ultraviolet and green
44 Light blue–green filters out red and ultraviolet
44A Light blue–green substracts red
45 Blue–green Mostly used in photomicrography, this contrast filter is designed to absorb ultraviolet and red
47 Blue is the filter used to give contrast effects with monochrome film. Also used for colour separation
47B Deep blue This filter is intended mainly for use in colour separation and tricolour printing
50 Deep blue is a monochromat filter (see *narrow band* filters) which transmits the mercury line at 436 nm, and lines at 398, 405 and 408 nm

Narrow band

These are *monochromat* filters which transmit very small parts of the spectrum — that is, just one hue. As a result, they are very dense and are only used for technical purposes. The most common use for narrow-band, or *narrow cut* filters is in colour separation work, particularly when the separation negatives are being made from transparencies or negatives.

70 Dark red This is used in colour separation work to produce separation positives from colour negatives. It is also used when making colour prints with the tricolour printing method
72B Dark orange–yellow
74 Dark green This transmits only 10 per cent of green light and filters out practically all yellow light from mercury-vapour lamps. This gives monochromatic green light which is useful in experimental optical work as the principal focus, in lenses corrected for one colour, is computed for green light
75 Dark blue–green

Filtering for effect *The windmill shot (above, left) was taken on colour infrared film. If no filtration is used this film tends to give results which are very blue. You can use a variety of filters to cut down the amount of blue light, including yellow, orange, red and opaque types. In this case an orange filter was used. The black and white shot was taken on normal film, but a red filter was used to darken the sky and generally increase contrast.*

Conversion

These filters are used to convert daylight to tungsten, or vice versa. They are most commonly used on the camera lens, but they can be used over lights. For example, some photographers use the blue (80) filter over tungsten lights so that they can use them with daylight and daylight film (see picture on page 74). Use of these filters is dealt with separately.

80 series, blue These are used with daylight film in tungsten lighting. The complete range is: 80A, 80B, 80C
85 series, amber These are used with tungsten film in daylight. The complete range is: 85, 85B, 85BN6, 85C, 85N3, 85N6, 85N9 (includes 0.9 neutral density)

Light balancing

These are paler versions of the conversion filters, and are designed to modify colour temperature for minor corrections. They are nearly always placed over the camera lens. You can use them with conversion filters to give full correction for light sources such as domestic bulbs (see separate table) or to give slight overcorrection for creative effect.

81 series, pale amber These slightly lower the colour temperature. The range is: 81, 81A, 81B, 81C, 81D, 81EF
82 series, pale blue These slightly raise the effective colour temperature. The range is: 82, 82A, 82B, 82C

Balancing colour

If the colour temperature of a light source is 3200K or 3400K then you can use an 80 series filter with daylight film or, in the case of the latter figure, tungsten film. But it is rare that the light is exactly the right colour, so the table below shows you what extra filtration is needed to bring the colour to the above figures.

3200K from	3400K from	Filter	Exposure increase in stops
2490K	2610K	82C + 82C	1⅓
2570K	2700K	82C + 82B	1⅓
2650K	2780K	82C + 82A	1
2720K	2870K	82C + 82	1
2800K	2950K	82C	2/3
2900K	3060K	82B	2/3
3000K	3180K	82A	1/3
3100K	3290K	82	1/3
3300K	3510K	81	1/3
3400K	3630K	81A	1/3
3500K	3740K	81B	1/3
3600K	3850K	81C	2/3
3850K	4140K	81EF	2/3

Miscellaneous

These are filters which do not fit into any of the other categories. They are all intended for various technical applications but are worth knowing about in case you ever come across them.

87 Visually opaque There are two versions of this filter—87 and 87C. Their main use is for infrared work as they absorb all visible light but transmit infrared radiation. This means that the exposure is achieved solely with infrared which is useful for analytical work. And for creative photography it means that the strange effects casued by infrared are even more dramatic
88A Visually opaque Similar to the 87
89B Visually opaque This is also used for infrared photography, particularly aerial work. It transmits radiation of wavelengths between 700 and 800 nm
90 Dark greyish amber This filter is meant for visual use, not for taking pictures with. Looking through the filter, the view is monochromatic and this gives you an idea of how the tones and colours will reproduce on black and white film
92 Red This is used, with 93 and 94, to take densitometer readings of colour films and papers
93 Green Used, with 92 and 94, to take densitometer readings of colour films and papers
94 Blue Used, with 92 and 93, to take densitometer readings from colour films and papers
96 Neutral density See separate table
98 Blue Equivalent to a 47B plus a 2B. Used in colour separation work and tricolour printing
99 Green Equivalent to a 61 plus a 16. Used in colour separation work and tricolour printing

Warm tones *When using flash, the skin tones tend to reproduce slightly too cold. You can produce a much warmer and healthier effect by using an 81A (below)*

Light balance *If you want to have the controllability of tungsten lights but prefer to use daylight film you will have to use an 80 series filter (right)*

Fluorescent conversion

This table shows the filtration and exposure increase necessary to get acceptable results with different types of fluorescent tube. It is based on Kodak films, but with a little experimentation you can adapt it for other makes. In any case, the figures are only intended as a guide, and for critical results you should always make tests.

Type of tube	Daylight films Neg. films, Ektachrome 200 and Kodachrome 25	Ektachrome 64 and 400, Kodachrome 64	Tungsten films
Daylight	40M + 40Y + 1 stop	50M + 50Y + 1⅓ stops	85B + 40M + 30Y + 1⅔ stops
White	20C + 30M + 1 stop	40M + ⅔ stop	60M + 40Y + 1⅔ stops
Warm white	40C + 40M + 1⅓ stops	20C + 40M + 1 stop	50M + 40Y + 1 stop
Warm white deluxe	60C + 30M + 2 stops	60C + 30M + 2 stops	10M + 10Y + ⅔ stop
Cool white	30M + ⅔ stop	40M + 10Y + 1 stop	10R + 50M + 50Y + 1⅔ stops
Cool white deluxe	20C + 10M + ⅔ stop	20C + 10M + ⅔ stop	20M + 40Y ⅔ stop
Unknown	10B + 10M + ⅔ stop	30M + ⅔ stop	50R 1 stop

Neutral density

Neutral density (ND) filters have no effect on colour, but simply cut down the amount of light entering the lens, allowing you to use a larger stop, longer exposures or to take pictures of objects which are otherwise far too bright (such as the sun). The values listed are the strengths available using single filters, though other strengths can be obtained using combinations. The precise effects of these filters will vary depending on the conditions of use, as there will be reciprocity effects with long exposure times, so you should experiment.

Filter	Filter factor	Transmission (%)	Exposure increase in stops
0.1	1¼	80	⅓
0.2	1½	63	⅔
0.3	2	50	1
0.4	2½	40	1⅓
0.5	3	32	1⅔
0.6	4	25	2
0.7	5	20	2⅓
0.8	6	16	2⅔
0.9	8	13	3
1.0	10	10	3⅓
2.0	100	1	6⅔
3.0	1000	0.1	10
4.0	10,000	0.01	13⅓

Colour compensating (CC)

These filters are very useful for making slight modifications to colour temperature so that you can get the exact colour that you want. They can also be used to give slight colour casts for creative effect. And used in filter packs they can correct for unusual lighting, such as fluorescent (see separate table). When mentioned in tables or articles they are often written without the CC prefix. But in technical information and on the packets they come in, they carry the prefix shown in the table.

Cyan	CC05C	CC10C	CC20C	CC30C	CC40C	CC50C
exposure increase	⅓ stop	⅓ stop	⅓ stop	⅔ stop	⅔ stop	1 stop
Magenta	CC05M	CC10M	CC20M	CC30M	CC40M	CC50M
exposure increase	⅓ stop	⅓ stop	⅓ stop	⅔ stop	⅔ stop	⅔ stop
Yellow	CC05Y	CC10Y	CC20Y	CC30Y	CC40Y	CC50Y
exposure increase		⅓ stop	⅓ stop	⅓ stop	⅓ stop	⅔ stop
Red	CC05R	CC10R	CC20R	CC30R	CC40R	CC50R
exposure increase	⅓ stop	⅓ stop	⅓ stop	⅔ stop	⅔ stop	1 stop
Green	CC05G	CC10G	CC20G	CC30G	CC40G	CC50G
exposure increase	⅓ stop	⅓ stop	⅓ stop	⅔ stop	⅔ stop	1 stop
Blue	CC05B	CC10B	CC20B	CC30B	CC40B	CC50B
exposure increase	⅓ stop	⅓ stop	⅔ stop	⅔ stop	1 stop	1⅓ stop

PHOTO DATA

Hyperfocal distance

Any focal length lens has a range of hyperfocal distances—one for each aperture. The hyperfocal distance is that focus setting at which the lens will give the maximum depth of field at that aperture. This depth of field extends from half the hyperfocal distance to infinity and increases as the aperture becomes smaller.

The tables given below indicate the hyperfocal distances for various focal length lenses at different apertures. One of the tables is based on the standard circle of confusion of 0.033 mm, the other is based on a more critical 0.025 mm (see pages 962 to 963). To use the tables, look at the figure indicated for the focal length lens you are using, at the working aperture, and set this distance on the lens. For example, if you are using a 35 mm lens at an aperture of *f*/5.6 you can, by setting the focus to 6.62 m, achieve acceptable sharpness from 3.31 m to infinity.

c × *0·033 mm*

Focal length / Aperture	17	21	24	28	35	50	85	100	135	200	300
1·4	6·25	9·54	12·40	16·90	26·50	54·10	156	216	394	856	1948
2	4·37	6·68	8·72	11·80	18·50	37·80	109	151	276	606	1363
2·8	3·12	4·77	6·23	8·48	13·20	27·00	78·1	108	197	432	974
4	2·18	3·34	4·36	5·93	9·28	18·90	54·7	75·7	138	303	681
5·6	1·56	2·38	3·11	4·24	6·62	13·50	39·0	54·1	98·6	206	487
8	1·09	1·67	2·18	2·96	4·64	9·46	27·3	37·8	69·0	151	340
11	0·79	1·21	1·58	2·15	3·37	6·88	19·9	27·5	50·2	110	247
16	0·54	0·83	1·09	1·48	2·32	4·73	13·6	18·9	34·5	75·7	170
22	0·39	0·60	0·79	1·07	1·68	3·44	9·95	13·6	25·1	55·0	123
32	0·27	0·41	0·54	0·74	1·16	2·36	6·84	9·95	17·2	37·8	85·2

c × *0·025 mm*

Aperture	17	21	24	28	35	50	85	100	135	200	300
1·4	8·25	12·6	16·4	22·4	35	71·4	206	285	520	1142	2571
2	5·78	8·82	11·5	15·6	24·5	50	144	200	364	800	1800
2·8	4·12	6·3	8·22	11·2	17·5	35·7	103	142	260	571	1285
4	2·89	4·41	5·76	7·84	12·2	25	72·2	100	182	400	900
5·6	2·06	3·15	4·11	5·6	8·75	17·8	51·6	71·4	130	285	642
8	1·44	2·20	2·88	3·92	6·12	12·5	36·1	50	91·1	200	450
11	1·05	1·60	2·09	2·85	4·45	9·09	26·2	36·3	66·2	145	327
16	0·72	1·10	1·44	1·96	3·06	6·25	18·0	25	45·5	100	225
22	0·52	0·80	1·04	1·42	2·22	4·54	13·1	18·1	33·1	72·7	163
32	0·36	0·55	0·72	0·98	1·53	3·12	9·03	12·5	22·7	50	112

Close-up exposure increase

When a camera is used for close-up work with the lens mounted on extension tubes or bellows, the *f*-stop markings no longer give an accurate indication of the amount of light reaching the film. Cameras with TTL metering will automatically compensate for this but for manual cameras it is necessary to refer to formulae or tables to calculate the additional exposure requred. Given below are two formulae and a reference table covering most common set-ups.

Estimating magnification can also be difficult. On a 5 × 4 camera, it is possible to measure both the size of the subject and the size of the image on the ground glass screen and so work out the magnification. With 35 mm cameras, the full frame dimensions of 24 × 36 mm give you a basis for calculation. With reproductions of life size or larger, working from the formulae will give optimum accuracy.

$$\text{Required exposure time} = \text{indicated meter exposure} \times \frac{(\text{length of bellows})^2}{(\text{lens focal length})^2}$$

$$\text{Required exposure time} = \text{indicated meter exposure} \times (m + 1)^2$$

Magnification	0·25	0·5	0·75	1	1·25	1·5	1·75	2	3
exposure factor	1·5	2·2	3	4	5	6·5	7·5	9	16

Sharpness control *The lens used for the seascape shot was focused at its hyperfocal distance in order to gain the maximum possible depth of field, extending all the way to infinity. Depth of field in close-up work is much more limited, as shown in the picture of a printed circuit board (far right), so it is essential to use the shallow sharpness creatively, to emphasize part of the subject*

Reciprocity failure compensation

In normal use the speed and colour balance of a film remains unchanged. For example, two shots taken at 1/125 second at *f*/4 and 1/250 second at *f*/5.6 of the same subject under the same conditions will have the same density and colour balance. When exposures get very short (1/10,000 second or less) or long (more than one second) the film reacts differently and adjustments have to be made by means of filters and extra exposure. The following table gives some recommended adjustments for the most popular Kodak films. For other films you should experiment, basing your tests on the nearest type of film given below. Alternatively obtain information from the film's manufacturer.

Film	Exposure time (seconds) 1/1000	1/100	1/10	1	10	100
EKTACHROME 64 Professional (Daylight)	None No filter	None No filter	None No filter	+ 1 stop CC 15B	+ 1½ stops CC 20B	Not recommended
EKTACHROME 160 and 160 Professional (Tungsten)	None No filter	None No filter	None No filter	+ ½ stop CC 10R	Not recommended	Not recommended
EKTACHROME 400 (Daylight)	None No filter	None No filter	None No filter	+ ½ stop No filter	+ 1½ stops CC 10C	+ 2½ stops CC 10C
EKTACHROME 50 Professional (Tungsten)	+ ½ stop CC 10G	None No filter	None No filter	None No filter	+ 1 stop CC 20B	Not recommended
EKTACHROME 200 and 200 Professional (Daylight)	None No filter	None No filter	None No filter	+ ½ stop CC 10R	+ 1 stop CC 15R	Not recommended
KODACOLOR 400	None No filter	None No filter	None No filter	+ ½ stop No filter	+ 1 stop No filter	+ 2 stops No filter
KODACHROME 25 (Daylight)	None No filter	None No filter	None No filter	+ 1 stop CC 10M	+ 1½ stops CC 10M	+ 2½ stops CC 10M
KODACHROME 64 (Daylight)	None No filter	None No filter	None No filter	+ 1 stop CC 10R	Not recommended	Not recommended

Close-up depth of field

Calculating depth of field is often important but never more so than in close-up work where the depth of field available at the working aperture is likely to be both small and very important. It is possible to make rough visual checks on depth of field at different apertures with most SLR and large format cameras but the darkened screen makes such estimates both difficult and crude. For crucial work it is best to refer to a table. The tables printed here show the depth of field available at different apertures and magnifications/reproduction ratios. One of the tables is based on a standard circle of confusion of 0.033 mm—the other uses a figure of 0.025 mm and is recommended for more critical work. In both cases the figures give the depth each side of the main focus—for total depth of field in mm double the figures.

c = 0·033 mm

Mag.	0·1	0·13	0·17	0·2	0·25	0·33	0·5	0·67	1	1·5	2	2·5	3
ratio	1·10	1·8	1·6	1·5	1·4	1·3	1·2	2·3	1·1	3·2	2·1	5·2	3·1
1·4	5·08	3·08	1·87	1·38	0·92	0·56	0·27	0·17	0·092	0·051	0·034	0·025	0·02
2	7·26	4·41	2·67	1·98	1·32	0·08	0·39	0·24	0·13	0·073	0·049	0·036	0·029
2·8	10·1	6·17	3·74	2·77	1·84	1·12	0·55	0·34	0·18	0·10	0·069	0·051	0·041
4	14·5	8·82	5·34	3·96	2·64	1·61	0·79	0·49	0·26	0·14	0·099	0·073	0·058
5·6	20·3	12·3	7·48	5·54	3·69	2·25	1·10	0·68	0·36	0·2	0·13	0·1	0·082
8	29	17·6	10·46	7·92	5·28	3·22	1·58	0·98	0·52	0·29	0·14	0·14	0·11
11	39·9	24·2	14·6	10·8	7·26	4·43	2·17	1·35	0·72	0·4	0·2	0·2	0·16
16	58	35·3	21·3	15·8	10·5	6·44	3·16	1·96	1·05	0·58	0·29	0·29	0·23
22	79·8	48·5	29·3	21·7	14·5	8·26	4·35	2·7	1·45	0·08	0·4	0·4	0·32
32	116	70·6	42·7	31·6	21·1	12·8	6·33	3·92	2·11	1·17	0·59	0·59	0·46
45	163	99·2	60·1	44·5	29·7	18·1	8·91	5·52	2·97	1·65	0·83	0·83	0·66
64	232	141	85·5	63·3	42·2	25·7	12·6	7·85	4·22	2·34	1·18	1·18	0·93

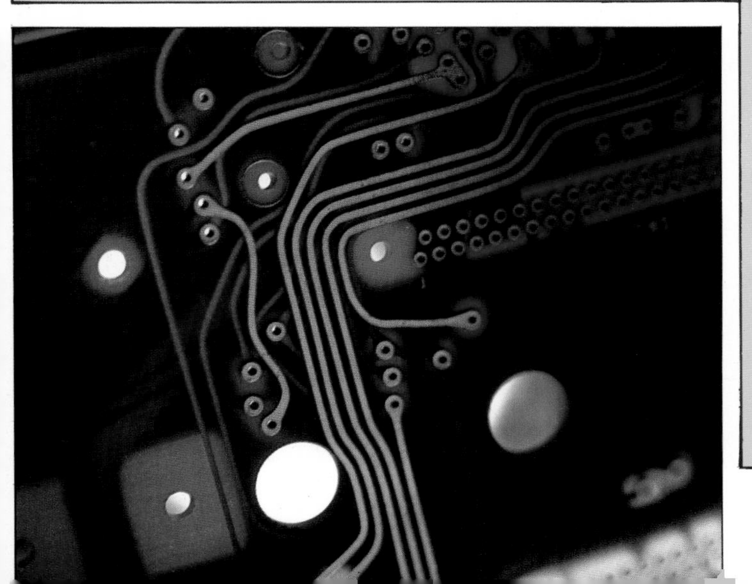

c = 0·025 mm

Mag.	0·1	0·13	0·17	0·2	0·25	0·33	0·5	0·67	1	1·5	2	2·5	3
ratio	1·10	1·8	1·6	1·5	1·4	1·3	1·2	2·3	1·1	3·2	2·1	5·2	3·1
1·4	3·85	2·34	1·41	1·05	0·7	0·42	0·21	0·13	0·07	0·038	0·026	0·019	0·015
2	5·5	3·34	2·02	1·5	1	0·61	0·3	0·18	0·1	0·055	0·037	0·028	0·022
2·8	7·7	4·68	2·83	2·1	1·4	0·85	0·42	0·26	0·14	0·077	0·052	0·039	0·031
4	11	6·68	4·04	3	2	1·22	0·6	0·37	0·2	0·11	0·075	0·056	0·044
5·6	15·4	9·36	5·66	4·2	2·8	1·7	0·84	0·52	0·28	0·15	0·1	0·078	0·062
8	22	13·3	8·09	6	4	2·44	1·2	0·74	0·4	0·22	0·15	0·11	0·088
11	30·2	18·3	11·1	8·25	5·5	3·35	1·65	1·02	0·55	0·3	0·2	0·15	0·12
16	44	26·7	16·1	12	8	4·88	2·4	0·48	0·8	0·44	0·3	0·22	0·17
22	60·5	36·7	22·2	16·5	11	6·71	3·3	2·04	1·1	0·61	0·41	0·3	0·24
32	88	53·4	32·3	24	16	9·77	4·8	2·97	1·6	0·88	0·6	0·44	0·35
45	123	75·2	45·5	33·7	22·5	13·7	6·75	4·18	2·25	1·25	0·84	0·71	0·63
64	176	100	64·7	48	32	19·5	9·6	5·95	3·2	1·77	1·2	0·89	0·71

Flash guide numbers

It is essential to know the guide number of your flashgun but manufacturers do not always quote a full set of numbers. By using this table you can work out the guide number of a flashgun at any of the given film speeds, provided that you know one number. For example, if your unit has a guide number of 22 with 64 ASA (ISO) film, simply look down the 64 ASA column until you come to 22. Then, by reading along that row, you can find the number for the other speeds. In this example the unit has a guide number of 40 with 200 ASA film.

The BCPS (beam candle power seconds) rating is a standard measure of light power and is useful for technical applications, such as infrared photography. The joules rating is a more common system of giving the power of a unit, and the power of most studio flash heads is quoted in joules

25	50	64	80	100	160	200	400	BCPS	Joules (watt/seconds)
6	9	10	11	12	16	18	25	300	8
7	10	11	12	14	18	20	28	375	10
8	11	12	14	16	20	22	32	450	12
9	12	14	16	18	22	25	35	600	16
10	14	16	18	20	25	28	40	750	20
11	16	18	20	22	28	32	45	900	25
12	18	20	22	25	32	35	50	1200	32
14	20	22	25	28	35	40	56	1500	40
16	22	25	28	32	40	45	64	1800	50
18	25	28	32	35	45	50	70	2400	64
20	28	32	35	40	50	56	80	3000	80
22	32	35	40	45	56	63	90	3600	100
25	35	40	45	50	63	70	100	4800	125
28	40	45	50	56	70	80	113	6000	160
32	45	50	56	63	80	90	128	7200	200

Sources

Much of the information used in this article was supplied by Kodak. Many of the terms used, such as Wratten, Ektachrome and Kodachrome are Kodak trade names. The hyperfocal distance and depth of field tables were calculated using a Sinclair ZX Spectrum computer.

Colour temperature and mireds

If you want to get accurate colours in your transparencies it is essential to filter for different light sources. Working out the required filtration is easy if you have a colour temperature meter. Otherwise it is difficult to know what colour temperature a particular light source is. The table here gives a guide to the most common or important sources, measured in kelvins. However, the exact colour of any lighting can be affected by the age of bulbs or tubes, the colour of reflectors or surrounding surfaces, and so on. Nevertheless, for all but the most critical conditions, this guide should be sufficiently accurate.

To find the necessary filtration you can use the kelvin/mired scale. Mireds (micro reciprocal degrees) are used because a filter can then be given a set value which applies to any region of the colour temperature range. For example, a filter with a mired shift value of −100 can change the colour temperature from 2000 to 2500 K—a shift of 500 K. But it can also change it from 5000 to 10,000 K—a shift of 5000 K. So filters cannot simply be allotted a colour temperature. The mired scale is derived by dividing the colour temperature into 1,000,000. Blue filters have negative mired values, and red, yellow and amber filters have positive values. Some colour temperature meters, such as the Minolta digital model, give readouts directly in mired values, which are then read off a table to find the correct filters to use. Some approximate mired values are given here for the most common filters, but you should check with the filter's instructions. The point to remember about mireds is that a filter alters the mired value by the same amount whatever the light source, but the change in degrees kelvin varies with the colour temperature of the light.

Source	K
Candle	1930
Sunrise/sunset	c. 2000
40 watt domestic bulb	2650
75 watt domestic bulb	2820
100 watt domestic bulb	2900
200 watt domestic bulb	2980
500 watt photographic lamp	3200
Projector lamps	3100
500 watt photoflood	3400
'Daylight' fluorescent light	4500
Mean noon sunlight	5400
Photographic daylight	5500
Flashcube	5500
Blue flashbulb	6000
Electronic flash tube	6000
Average daylight (sun and sky)	6500
Colour matching fluorescent tube	6500
Overcast daylight	7500
Blue sky	10,000 to 18,000

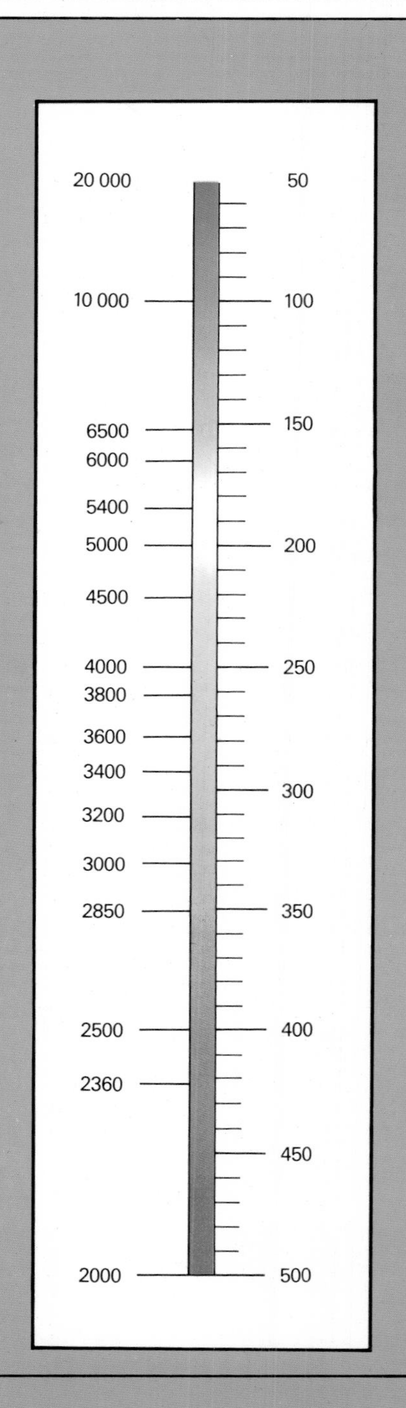

Mired values for common filters

Filter	Mired	Filter	Mired
81	+ 10	82	− 10
81A	+ 15	82A	− 20
81B	+ 25	82B	− 30
81C	+ 30	80A	− 130
85B	+ 130	80B	− 110
85C	+ 80	80C	− 80

INDEX

Numbers in italics refer to illustrations